The Careless QUILTER

The Careless QUILTER

DECIDE-AS-YOU-SEW, DESIGN-AS-YOU-GO QUILTMAKING

Kristin Miller

RUTLEDGE HILL PRESS
Nashville, Tennessee

Published in Nashville, Tennessee, by Rutledge Hill Press, Inc.
211 Seventh Avenue North, Nashville, Tennessee 37219

Typography by D&T/Bailey, Inc., Nashville, Tennessee
Design by Harriette Bateman

Library of Congress Cataloging-in-Publication Data

Miller, Kristin, 1946–
      The careless quilter : decide as you sew, design as you go
  quiltmaking / by Kristin Miller.
          p.   cm.
      Includes index.
      ISBN 1-55853-296-X
      1. Patchwork.   2. Patchwork quilts.   I. Title.
  TT835.M517   1994
  746.9'7 — dc20   94-7377
                                                            CIP

Printed in the United States of America
1 2 3 4 5 6 7 8 9 — 99 98 97 96 95 94

To my parents

I grew up watching my mother and
father make beautiful and useful
things, and it seemed natural that I
could create objects of beauty and
utility too.

PHOTOGRAPHS BY: Stewart Brinton, Peggy
Carl, Susan Earl, Brian Gauvin, Viviann Kuehl,
Iain Lawrence, Gordon McCaw, Marie Meynen,
Kristin Miller, Loomis Miller, Margaret Miller,
Julie Moore, Lee Oates, and Nancy Robertson.

Black and white photographs by Nancy
Robertson, except 6-36 by Kristin Miller.

Color photographs as follows:
Stewart Brinton: 30, 40.
Peggy Carl: 33, 58.
Susan Earl: 37.
Brian Gauvin: 24.
Viviann Kuehl: 12, 20, 42.
Iain Lawrence: 34, 36.
Gordon McCaw: 6, 9, 14, 16, 44, 51, 52.
Marie Meynen: 54–56.
Kristen Miller: 19, 31.
Loomis Miller: 43.
Margaret Miller: 25, 32.
Julie Moore: 1–5, 7, 11, 13, 15, 18, 21, 22, 27–
    29, 35, 38, 39, 45–49, 53, 57.
Lee Oates: 8, 10, 17, 23, 26, 41, 50.

DRAWINGS BY Kristin Miller.

Quilts featured in this book are by Kristin Miller
unless otherwise noted.

Some of the material in this book had its origin in
articles for *Threads, Quilt World, Quilt, Country
Quilts, Quilt Almanac,* and *Progress.*

Contents

Acknowledgments

I thank the many friends who were interested and encouraging during the long process of writing this book, especially Iain, who patiently dealt with computer frustrations, critiqued my writing, and helped with difficult drawings. I thank my mother for proofreading the manuscript and for giving thoughtful and gentle criticism.

I am extremely grateful to the many photographers who took pictures for me. Especially appreciated are Nancy Robertson, who followed my every whim in doing the how-to photos, and Julie Moore, whose patience and attention to detail were a revelation.

Introduction

The many choices involved in quiltmaking can be overwhelming. The decisions to be made before you can even begin sewing may seem the most difficult. Armed with graph paper and colored pencils, you wrestle with the task of getting your dream quilt down on paper. Several frustrating hours later, you decide to follow a pattern from a quilt magazine, making a quilt just like the one in the picture.

If you are tired of graph paper and fed up with precise measuring, if you find it hard to be as careful and persnickety as most quilt books expect, perhaps you should try a different approach. If you are panicking because your quilt is not turning out perfectly despite your best efforts, if you are bored with copying yet scared to make your own designs, you might enjoy a more spontaneous method of quiltmaking, using decide-as-you-sew techniques that make it easy and fun to be creative.

Decide-as-you-sew methods appeal to the many people who are neither patient nor careful by nature, to those with a somewhat haphazard approach to creativity, to the easily frustrated, and to quiltmakers who have grown bored with traditional methods. This is not a book for the perfectionist, but for the rest of us.

Design Your Quilt As You Sew It

Designing a quilt can be an ongoing process, with design and fabric decisions being made as the quilt is being sewn. Using the decide-as-you-sew medallion method presented here, you can make a progression of small choices as your quilt grows outward from the center in a series of concentric borders sewn on one after another. You don't need to plan or graph your design; you don't even need to picture what the finished quilt will look like.

At its simplest, a design decision for a border involves choosing fabric, determining the width of the border, and deciding whether to construct it with strips or with triangles. The design becomes more intricate and elaborate when smaller patchwork pieces are used to form patterns within the strips or triangles that form the border.

The order and complexity of the borders can be varied endlessly to create a unique quilt of great beauty. But no matter how complicated a medallion quilt looks, if it is constructed in concentric borders, the design decisions can be made in a series of small, ongoing steps as the quilt develops.

I was not over fond of sewing, but I thought it best to begin my quilt early. So I collected a few squares of calico, and undertook to put them together in my usual independent way, without asking direction.

—Lucy Larcom, 1889

9

I-1. *Imagine that you have created a patchwork square.*

I-2. *Surround the square with four triangles.*

"Careless" Quiltmaking

I titled my book *The Careless Quilter*, not because I believe in sloppy workmanship, but because I believe there are a lot of people like myself who want to make quilts but who find the precise, exact instructions in most quilt books intimidating and uninviting. We are not all meticulous and painstaking by nature, and some of us would give up quiltmaking if we had to be.

From my very first quilt, I made a lot of mistakes, and I quickly learned it doesn't really matter. Mistakes can be corrected, ignored, or accepted. I corrected technical mistakes like fraying seam allowances or loose tension. Other mistakes, like corners that did not meet exactly, I often ignored. But I learned to accept and sometimes to welcome the really big mistakes as opportunities for creativity and originality.

Usually a mistake in patchwork is not a disaster. It is a new direction, a change of plan. When I sew the wrong triangles together, it gives me a new possibility to consider. Running short on one fabric means I add another that complements it. When I sew on a patchwork unit upside down, it changes the design, but not necessarily for the worse.

Process, Not Project

There is safety in the craft project approach to quiltmaking where color, pattern, and size are already decided for you. If you follow the instructions,

I-3. *Now try strips of fabric instead.*

I-4. *Fold strips in half for a narrower border.*

10

I-5. *Use triangles to form a cross.*

I-6. *Cut triangles in half and reposition to create a star.*

you don't have to make decisions, thus avoiding the possibility of making the wrong choice. But this approach may also be boring and restrictive, keeping you from discovering that there is not one correct answer, but a great variety of beautiful solutions.

The focus of *The Careless Quilter* is on the processes that will enable you to create your own patchwork designs, not on projects for you to copy. Instead of duplicating the quilts in this book, use them for ideas and inspiration.

Let's Imagine

Perhaps you are uncertain whether the decide-as-you-sew method is for you. Let's use an imaginary medallion to show you how the method works. Pretend that you made a patchwork square (See Photo I-1).

You decide to surround the square with a floral batik, so you cut out four triangles of fabric and place them around the square (Photo I-2).

But before you sew on the four

triangles, you want to try other possibilities. Remove the four triangles, and arrange four strips of fabric around the square instead (Photo I-3).

The effect of such a broad border is a little overwhelming, so fold each strip in half lengthwise to see the effect of a narrower border (Photo I-4).

To see what a patchwork border would look like, cut out a number of small triangles and lay them around the square to form a broad cross (Photo I-5).

I-7. *Slight rearrangement gives a sense of motion.*

I-8. *Changing patterns emerge as you experiment.*

Remove the triangles, cut each one in half, and rearrange them around the square. Now you have a star (Photo I-6).

See the possibilities? A different arrangement of the triangles creates a subtly different pattern, one with a strong sense of motion (Photo I-7).

Yet another rearrangement of the triangles around the square forms a stairstep pattern (Photo I-8).

As you play with the triangles, more and more design options emerge. Which one will you choose? There is no right or wrong; one design is not necessarily better than another. What is important is your own response to the varying patterns. Which one do *you* like best?

Use this process in border after border, experimenting, changing, arranging and rearranging, making the choices that please you most. Imagine the beautiful quilt you can make without patterns, without copying, and with little frustration.

How to Use This Book

Many of the illustrations show the development of a medallion as it grows over a period of time. These illustrations are clues to the processes that created the quilts. They are not meant to be instructions for copying the quilts; as you will notice, no measurements, dimensions, or patterns are given. Rather than copying the quilts shown here, use the examples as inspiration for creating your own.

If you are interested in straightforward "how-to" instructions, consult the chapters "Tools and Techniques," "How a Quilt Is Built," "Don't Quit Till It's Quilted," and "Troubleshooting."

The Careless QUILTER

Making Mistakes, Making Choices

The Amish and Mennonites are said to put a deliberate mistake into every quilt, to avoid rivaling God's perfection. I've never found this to be a problem: my quilts are a progression of mistakes. I've come to accept this as a natural and even beneficial aspect of my quiltmaking technique, and often as a source of creativity.

A mistake, which in patchwork usually means sewing the wrong things together, can often be a springboard to an intriguing new design. Mistakes should suggest new directions, new design possibilities, new choices. Accepting mistakes and making changes and choices as you sew will guarantee a unique and original quilt, and one more likely to be beautiful than boring.

It's Easy to Make Mistakes

Let's imagine that you're making a baby quilt just like the one pictured in your favorite quilt magazine. You've cut out the sixteen patterned and sixteen plain triangles that will form the four pinwheels in the center of the quilt (See Illustration 1-1).

Your first mistake is that you cut

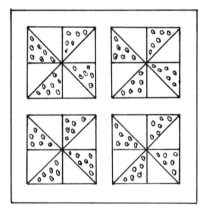

1-1. *Thirty-two small triangles compose the four pinwheels in a quilt's center.*

out all the triangles an inch larger than the directions specified. However, you leave them, and are even pleased that the quilt will be a little bigger than planned.

But your next mistake is more serious. You are supposed to sew the triangles together on their long edges so they look like Illustration 1-2.

1-2. *Triangles should be sewn together on their long edges.*

The man who makes no mistakes does not usually make anything.

—Bishop W. C. Magee

Instead, you sew them on their short edges so they look like Illustration 1-3.

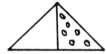

1-3. *Instead, you sew the short edges together!*

Even worse, you don't always choose the same short edge, so eight of the patchwork units have their triangles switched (Illustration 1-4).

1-4. *Now you realize that eight of the patchwork units have their triangles switched. Don't panic! The units can be used this way.*

Difficult Choices

Now you really have some difficult choices to make. You can get out the seam ripper and tear apart those carefully sewn "mistakes." You can throw the whole project in the back of the closet or give the pieces to the rummage sale. You can buy a different gift for the baby shower.

Or, you can change your ideas about what you're making and how you're making it. You can begin to think of these mistakes as the raw material for experimenting and creating a design of your own, instead of copying someone else's and getting upset when it doesn't turn out the same.

I suggest a more accepting attitude toward mistakes. If you can think of patchwork as a process, as a series of choices, and if you can incorporate your mistakes instead of throwing them away, you may find quiltmaking less frustrating and more exciting.

Try Experimenting

Create more elaborate shapes and patterns by combining your triangles in different ways. If you lay out your triangles on the table and start moving them around to form different patterns, you will soon see that there are a great number of possibilities. Before you sew, play with the triangles to see how many different designs you can invent.

Form a square or a diamond (Illustration 1-5).

Build a bigger triangle (Illustration 1-6).

Combine triangles to form patchwork strips and borders (Illustration 1-7).

Frame a square (Illustration 1-8).

Create a more elaborate triangle (Illustration 1-9).

Rediscover the pinwheel (Illustration 1-10).

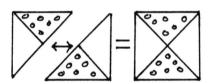

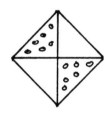

1-5. *Place the triangular patchwork units to form a square or a diamond.*

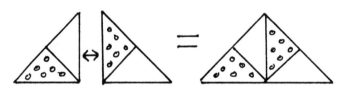

1-6. *Build a bigger triangle.*

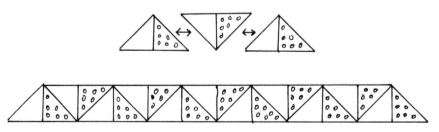

1-7. *Triangular units form patchwork strips and borders.*

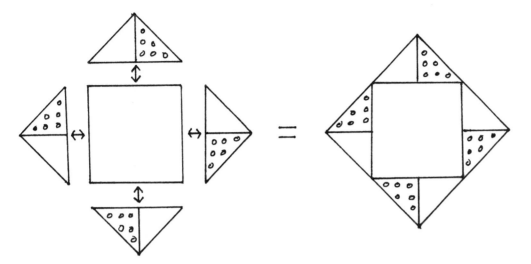

1-8. *Triangular units frame a square.*

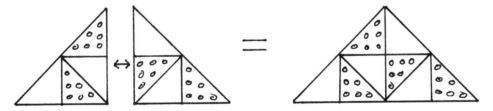

1-9. *Create a more elaborate triangle.*

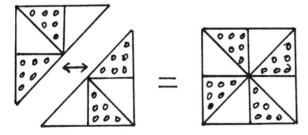

1-10. *Rediscover the pinwheel.*

Add other fabrics to increase design possibilities (Illustration 1-11).

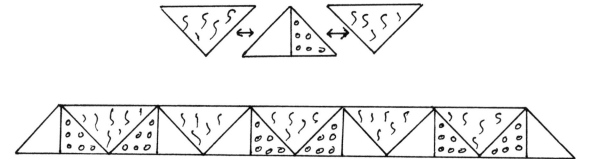

1-11. *Add other fabrics to increase design possibilities.*

Change the orientation to create new patterns (Illustration 1-12).

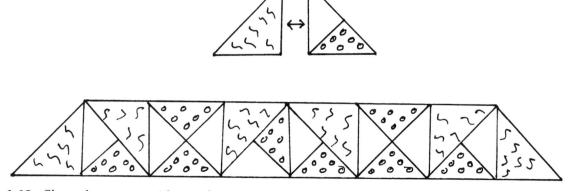

1-12. *Change the orientation of the triangles to create new patterns.*

Possibilities and Choices

You can see by now that an endless number of possible patterns and designs can develop. It's time now to make your first choices and begin your quilt. Instead of making a traditional block-by-block quilt, you might like to create a medallion quilt, using the elaborate triangles and patchwork strips you have invented.

Medallion Quilts

Medallion quilt construction methods may offer the most scope for inventive use of the many design com- binations you discovered by experi- menting with the triangles. Here are some possibilities.

Put Triangles Around

Start with the pinwheel and sur- round it with contrasting triangles (Il- lustration 1-13).

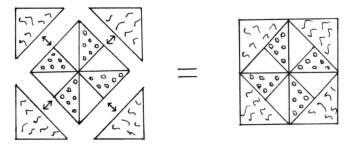

1-13. *Surround the pinwheel with contrasting triangles.*

Use Narrow Strips of Fabric to Frame the Medallion

A frame of contrasting design or color will dramatize the center square (Illustration 1-14).

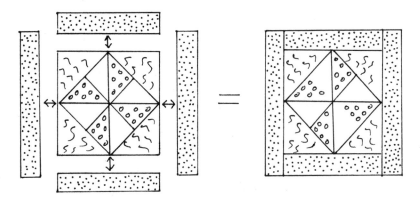

1-14. *Contrasting patterns or colors frame the center square.*

Add Fancy Patchwork Triangles

Surround the medallion with four bold patchwork triangles. By now, you will have used up the sixteen original triangular units and will need to make more (Illustration 1-15).

1-15. *Having used the sixteen original triangular units, you need to make more.*

Plain Triangles Quickly Enlarge the Quilt Top

The complexity of the central medallion is emphasized by the plain background (Illustration 1-16).

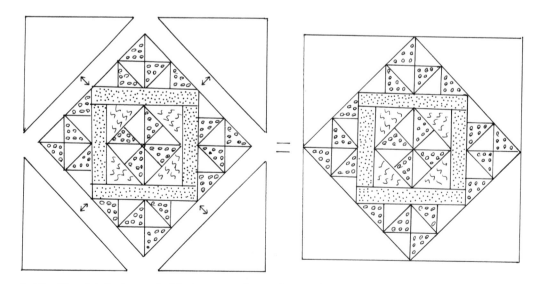

1-16. *The plain background of the large triangles emphasizes the complexity of the central medallion.*

Patchwork Borders Highlight the Design

Adding a fancy patchwork border (Illustration 1-17) surrounded by a frame of plain fabric strips (Illustration 1-18) creates a pleasing medallion.

Keep Going, to Make a Quilt

Working outward from the center, a series of concentric borders can be added to the growing medallion. Medallion patchwork is flexible and changeable. Border follows border until the quilt is big enough.

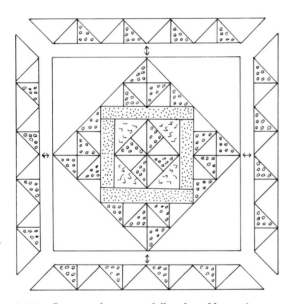

1-17. *Create a pleasing medallion by adding a fancy patchwork border.*

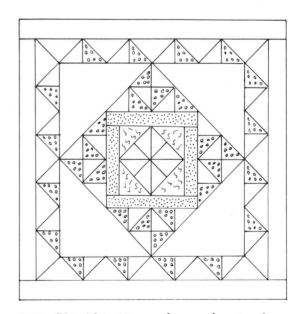

1-18. *Plain fabric strips provide a complementary frame.*

Turning Mistakes to Creative Advantage

If you sew something together in the wrong order, don't rip it apart immediately. Look at it first as a design possibility; you may like it better than what you had planned originally. These kinds of mistakes, especially in a design of small repetitive units, may add a very subtle and welcome asymmetry.

Even if you really need to correct a mistake, it is usually easier to cut and sew new pieces than to take out the seams and redo. Just be sure to save the discards. You may want to use them on something else later.

Although running out of a particular fabric may seem like a disaster, being forced to substitute a different fabric can jolt you toward a more dramatic or original design.

If you make a mistake and really don't like it, by all means correct it. Take it out, or sew something else over it. When I finish a quilt top, I hang it on the wall to look at it. Sometimes there will be a small part that doesn't please me, something that irritates my eyes. If it continues to bother me, I'll sew another piece over it with tiny hand stitches.

A great number of my medallions end up as potholders rather than as the quilts planned originally, because the designs weren't working out well enough to continue. But sometimes a potholder or wall hanging grows surprisingly into a beautiful quilt, because of unexpected changes and transformations.

Real Mistakes

The real mistakes in quiltmaking occur when you fail to take the time and care required to create an object of value, or when you use shoddy materials or such poor sewing techniques that your quilt doesn't last at least as long as you do.

It is a real mistake to have seams come apart because you used cheap thread or didn't bother to adjust the tension. It is a real mistake to spend months piecing together a quilt top, then skimp on the quilting.

It is a real mistake not to sign and date your work, if you are pleased with it. It is a real mistake to use fabric that you don't like, just to get rid of it.

It is a real mistake to throw away your mistakes. Save all patchwork pieces; what wasn't suited to one project may be exactly what is needed for the next, and your work will be half done. I have a "mistake basket" where I throw all unused patchwork units; when I am stuck, I look in the basket for quick inspiration.

The Biggest Mistake

The biggest mistake in quiltmaking is judging your work too harshly. You are bound to be disappointed in your quilt if you think it's no good just because it isn't perfect. A quilt can be constructed perfectly, yet be lackluster and lifeless. Another quilt may be flawed yet beautiful, its imperfections giving vibrancy and spirit. Sometimes perfect is boring. There is no right or wrong in quiltmaking, only a multitude of choices. And it's not a mistake to change your mind.

My Favorite Mistake

Like many previous craft projects, my first quilt started with a how-to article in a magazine. I didn't realize that the Blazing Star pattern might be a little difficult for a beginner.

I started out with enthusiasm, much too impatient to read — let alone follow — the complicated directions. In my haste, I cut out the pieces quite carelessly, and then had great trouble fitting them together. The seams wouldn't match. The bias-cut edges rippled and puckered in an alarming way. The color placement got mixed up.

By the second row of diamonds I was very frustrated: I knew there was no way I could handle the precise sewing together of 108 more diamonds, yet my patchwork star seemed radiantly beautiful to me. Instead of giving up, I appliquéd my careless star to a piece of denim and surrounded it with a print border of colorful butterflies, adding denim squares at the corners. I decided to make my own design instead of copying (See Plate 1, Yellow Butterfly, center detail).

I made four long patchwork strips out of small triangles and used these strips to frame my medallion. I made no attempt at all to match the designs at the corners, because I realized this was beyond my skill. Two floral borders completed the medallion.

I quilted my quilt with big awkward stitches that were the best I could do. Then I hung it on the wall and stepped back to look at it. It was far from perfect, yet it was surprisingly beautiful. I was proud and amazed at what I had created, by mistake (Plate 2, Yellow Butterfly).

Making Mistakes, Making Choices

Making mistakes and making choices are closely intertwined in my quiltmaking repertoire. The mistakes I made in my first quilt taught me the most important quiltmaking lesson: there are an infinite number of acceptable and exciting choices as a quilt is being created.

The Afternoon in Paradise quilt (Plate 3, Afternoon in Paradise) is much more complex and elaborate than the Yellow Butterfly quilt, and was made several years later. By then, making choices was the most interesting aspect of quiltmaking to me.

Arbitrary Choices

How does a complicated quilt begin? How does it grow and change? The Afternoon in Paradise quilt began with a pile of fabrics that I liked, and design decisions were made as I sewed. No measurements, no yardages, no coordinating colors, no designing, no planning ahead. Just a pile of fabrics, of pieces large and small, and a series of choices that were made as I sewed my quilt. Without prior planning, how did the design emerge?

Many quilters find it startling that I begin sewing a medallion without planning or designing the patchwork first. "How do you know what fabric to use?" they ask. "How do you know what will look right?"

I make my choices border by border, as the medallion grows outward from the center. I don't have to visualize the finished quilt; I just have to decide the next border.

In describing how the Afternoon in Paradise quilt was made, I hope to show the arbitrary nature of many of my design choices. Only by trying out a few of them can you find the one that pleases you the most.

Making a number of small, ongoing decisions is much less intimidat-

ing to me than having to plan the quilt beforehand. I can hold a potential fabric choice next to the medallion and see if it clicks. Instead of plotting it on graph paper, I watch the design reveal itself to me as it is created through small successive choices.

Experimental Medallions

I had gathered together a pile of fabric that interested me. There was shiny chintz paisley, scraps from a Hawaiian shirt, a snippet of Japanese kimono fabric, a cheap border print skirt from a rummage sale, some dainty calicoes, and a few geometric prints. My eyes couldn't stay away from a set of four big squares with splendidly colored flowers in a Slavic folk art style. I wanted those flowers in the middle of a medallion (Plate 4, Afternoon in Paradise, bottom medallion detail).

Often, when beginning a new project and excited by the fabric and the designs being created, I'll make three or four medallions with a similar theme. These medallions sometimes become parts of several different quilts and projects, or they may be combined together in one quilt, as happened here.

I don't worry about their eventual disposition as I make them. Instead I use the creation of these several medallions as an exercise, a warm-up, a pleasurable way to experiment and become acquainted with different design possibilities. I decided to experiment with the Slavic flowered squares.

Evolution of the Central Panel

Let's look at the medallion that became the center of the quilt. It begins

with the bright floral square, and is framed by an oddly patterned piece of upholstery fabric in slightly somber shades of navy and beige (Illustration 1-19).

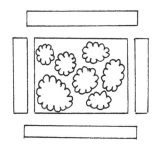

1-19. *The floral square is framed by plain fabric.*

How was this second fabric selected? Chosen fairly much at random, it was the one that "clicked" visually as I held several possibilities next to the center square. It certainly doesn't seem a likely choice, yet its presence so early in the quilt gave permission for other unusual fabrics to follow.

The dimensions of this border were decided partly by chance and partly by choice. Having only a small piece of this fabric, I chose to cut it into two narrow and two wider strips. Given the same piece of fabric, I could have cut all the strips the same width, or squeezed out four triangles, or saved it for later use.

Four beige corduroy trapezoids form the next border, flanked by patchwork triangles at the corners. The corduroy was chosen because it echoes the beige in the previous border, and because it exerts a calming effect after the visual complexity of the center. These trapezoids began as triangles, which were sewn to the four sides of the medallion. Finding the result uninspir-

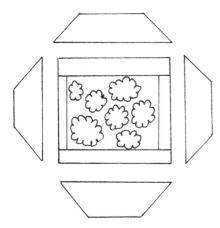

1-20. *Cutting off the tips of the triangles changes the medallion to an octagon.*

ing, I cut off the tips of the triangles, which changed the medallion to an octagonal shape (Illustration 1-20).

The octagon was returned to a square by adding four triangular patchwork units, constructed from smaller triangles.

These small triangles were cut from a Slavic floral square, a red-and-blue paisley, and a solid yellow fabric. Can you picture other fabrics that would have been suitable? Black triangles instead of yellow would have pointed more strongly toward the middle of the square. A small calico print instead of the large floral motif would

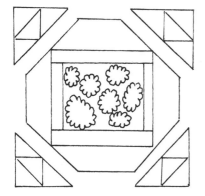

1-21. *Patchwork triangles return the octagonal medallion to a square.*

have given a more sedate air. Again, there are infinite possibilities, even if the choices are limited to those that echo the colors of the center square.

The patchwork triangles returned the octagonal medallion to a square (Illustration 1-21).

The next border is composed of four narrow strips of fabric (Illustration 1-22).

The dot-and-dash blue-and-white border has a strong visual impact, making the inner medallion vibrate against its surrounding background. A plain color or a more soothing pattern would have settled the medallion into the background more calmly (Plate 5, Afternoon in Paradise, inner medallion).

The quiet, beige corduroy reappears in the four large triangles that form a diamond around the medallion

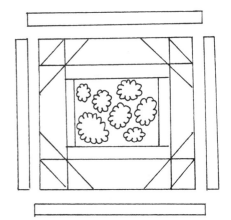

1-22. *Four narrow strips of fabric comprise the next border.*

(Illustration 1-23). As in the earlier corduroy border, these could have been trapezoids instead. Corduroy is a very matte fabric that absorbs rather than reflects light. Imagine a different fabric for this border, perhaps shiny satin.

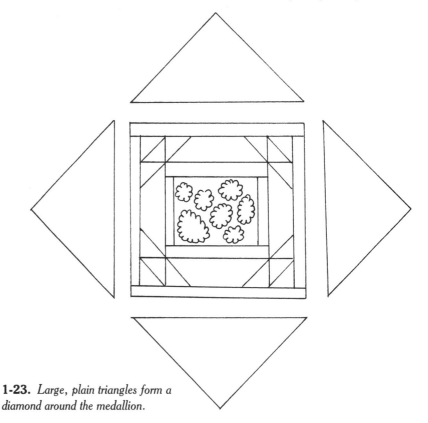

1-23. *Large, plain triangles form a diamond around the medallion.*

The diamond is outlined with a narrow border in a wild turquoise, black, and white Polynesian print (Illustration 1-24). The patterns on this fabric introduce a random note into the symmetry of the quilt, although the colors echo those used earlier. The peculiarity of this fabric was perhaps a gamble, but if it hadn't worked out, I could have sewn something else over this border to cover it up. But this weird fabric is what people tell me they like best about the quilt.

A wide border of yellow triangles repeats the yellow of the four small yellow triangles used earlier (Illustration 1-25).

1-24. *A narrow border of strips echoes colors found in the smaller triangles.*

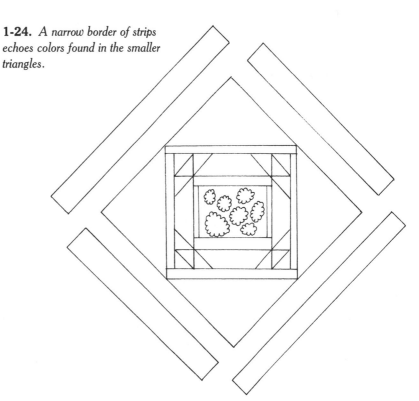

1-25. *Larger triangles repeat the color of the smaller triangles.*

This fabric was chosen for its cheery color, and because I had a big piece of it. By the time a quilt is this big, several yards of fabric are needed for the triangles. I happened to have three yards of yellow on hand. With a different choice of color, this "yellow" quilt could have been a pink or red or blue or beige quilt, thus altering its mood and ambiance.

A final border of old-fashioned pink-and-black latticework completes the central panel (Illustration 1-26).

Simultaneous Sewing

The top and bottom panels began experimentally; at the time I started them, they were not envisioned as part of the quilt. As mentioned earlier, I often work on several medallions at the same time, using similar fabrics, and decide later how to use them. The first several borders of the three medallions were all sewn fairly simultaneously. Only later did I decide to use one in the center and two in the top and bottom panels.

The Top Panel

The medallion that becomes the top panel begins with the Slavic floral square, surrounded by narrow strips of red paisley (Illustration 1-27).

Three strips of fabric on either side then elongate the medallion (Illustration 1-28). At this point I begin to imagine it as a fancy border at the top of the quilt.

I won't discuss other fabric choices in detail, as they were chosen with a similar philosophy as those of the center

1-26. *A final border completes the central panel.*

panel. If I had to state any guidelines for my choices, they would be to echo the colors in the floral squares, to repeat some of the fabrics used elsewhere in the quilt, and to be open and receptive to odd and unusual fabrics if they click visually.

Triangles are added to either end of the panel, changing its shape to a long hexagon (Illustration 1-29).

Strips of fabric are used log-cabin style to create chevron stripes that stretch the medallion further (Illustration 1-30).

Small triangles at the corners and a final strip of fabric at each end complete the panel (Illustration 1-31).

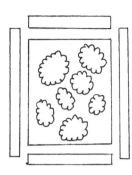

1-27. *The top panel medallion begins with a floral square, surrounded by narrow strips of fabric.*

1-28. *Three strips of fabric on either side elongate the medallion.*

1-29. *Triangles at both ends of the panel turn it into a long hexagon.*

1-30. *Chevron stripes stretch the medallion even further.*

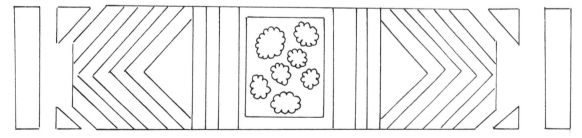

1-31. *Small triangles and a final strip of fabric complete the panel.*

The Bottom Panel

It would have been attractive to duplicate the top panel for the bottom panel, but by now I was really into playing around with the third experimental medallion, and decided to stretch it for the bottom panel.

Four Polynesian print triangles are joined to a floral square (Illustration 1-32).

1-32. *Four triangles are added to the floral square.*

Adding narrow trapezoidal strips of fabric creates an octagon (Illustration 1-33).

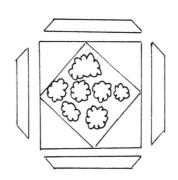

1-33. *Trapezoidal strips create an octagon.*

Narrow strips of fabric are sewn to two sides of small triangles to form patchwork triangles, which are added to either end of the medallion to change the shape to a hexagon (Illustration 1-34).

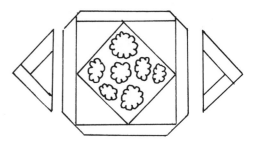

1-34. *Adding triangles on two ends changes the shape to a hexagon.*

Again, strips of fabric create chevron stripes to lengthen the hexagon, and triangles in the corners bring the shape back to a rectangle (Illustration 1-35).

1-35. *Strips of fabric and triangular corners bring the shape back to a rectangle.*

A number of strips of fabric are sewn together. Adding these sewn-together strips to either end of the medallion completes the bottom panel (Illustration 1-36).

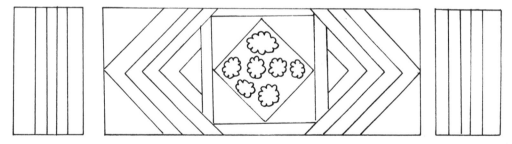

1-36. *Sewn-together strips complete the bottom panel.*

The top and bottom panels are then sewn to the center medallion.

The Final Outer Borders

A final set of borders frames the finished quilt (Illustration 1-37).

The fabric strips at the very top and bottom of the quilt are from the same border-print yardage, but have different motifs. The side borders, which bracket the quilt, also are dissimilar. These choices were made of necessity; I didn't have enough of any one fabric to make matching borders.

But I was pleased with the result.

As described in the chapter "Don't Quit Till It's Quilted," the quilting of the Afternoon in Paradise quilt was done in a similar spirit, with decisions on what and where to stitch being made as the quilting progressed.

29

1-37. *A final set of borders frames the finished quilt.*

Tools and Techniques

2

I would add a good sharp pair of scissors and a fifty-cent plastic triangle to Mrs. Watson's quilting necessities. Expensive devices are not essential to quiltmaking. A beautiful quilt can be made with simple and inexpensive tools. Scissors, needle, and thread are basic, but there are a few other items you might find useful.

Measuring and marking tools, sewing supplies, and workspace are discussed below. Quilting frames and supplies are described in the chapter "Don't Quit Till It's Quilted."

Tools and Supplies

A *fine-tip felt pen* is useful for marking accurate cutting lines. I prefer indelible ink because it won't run when the quilt is washed. Tailor's chalk can be used instead, but it will make a broader line. It's a good idea to do all marking on the backside of the fabric.

A *yardstick* does double duty in measuring and as a guide for drawing long, straight lines. A thin metal one is best, because you can get the tip of the felt pen right to the very edge of it. A ruler and a cloth measuring tape are handy, but not absolutely necessary.

Homemade or commercial *templates* are used for marking other shapes for patchwork pieces. An accurate square is handy, but perhaps you should obtain hexagons, diamonds, octagons, or other shapes only if you need them.

The *right-angle (ninety-degree) isosceles triangle* (with two sides equal in length) is a basic shape in medallion patchwork, and you will need a way to draw an accurate triangle. It's helpful to have several of these inexpensive plastic triangles (sold in stationery stores) in different sizes as they are the templates used most frequently in medallion patchwork.

The directions given in the next section for drawing your own cardboard templates can be used to make right-angle isosceles triangles in a number of sizes.

ARDCO™ templates are useful, precise metal templates with a nonslip backing. They were designed by an engineer and are sold in quilt shops.

A convenient template for drawing squares is made by the Yours Truly™ Company. It has slots for marking squares of different sizes (See Illustration 2-1).

With a little knowledge of geometry, templates can be made out of cardboard, but you will need to be *very* accurate in marking and cutting the shape. If you have a commercial template, you can draw the same shape,

> ## You want to make a quilt? You got needle and thread? That's all you need.
>
> — Mrs. Ora Watson

2-1. *A template helps you draw squares.*

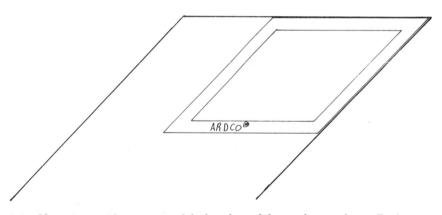

2-2. *Use a fine-tip felt pen to extend the lines beyond the template evenly on all sides.*

but in a larger size, by extending lines beyond the template and then tracing the template angles.

1. Draw two sides of the shape, extending the lines exactly the same number of inches on either side.

2. Move the template to the end of a line, trace the angle exactly, and extend the line beyond the template exactly the same number of inches as before (Illustration 2-2).

3. A line connecting the two open ends completes the shape.

An *L-shaped square* is an optional tool, but one I use frequently for marking lines, measuring, squaring up corners, checking right angles, and drawing large triangles. A large car-

penter's framing square is an extremely practical, though pricey, item.

The C-THRU™ Ruler Company makes a wonderful, inexpensive, plastic L-shaped square. Transparent and marked with a one-eighth-inch grid, it has innumerable uses in quilt-making. Look for it in stationery stores.

A *sewing machine* is optional, as it is perfectly possible to make a quilt without one. The patchwork quilt was invented well before the sewing machine, and there are still quilters who take pleasure in making quilts entirely by hand. I find a sewing machine fairly useless for quilting, but nearly indispensable for piecing together the patchwork top.

When using a machine, good quality polyester, cotton-covered polyester, or cotton thread can be used. Choose a needle size complimentary to the thread and fabric.

When sewing by hand, use a strong cotton thread; quilting thread works nicely for all patchwork. Wax the thread to prevent tangles. Don't use a huge needle, and do try a thimble. See the chapter "Don't Quit Till It's Quilted" for a more lengthy discussion of hand-sewing tools and techniques.

Sharp *scissors* are essential for precise cutting, so have scissors sharpened as often as necessary. If you are left-handed, a pair of left-handed scissors will make cutting faster and less frustrating.

Your good shears should be used for cutting fabric and thread *only*. Their sharpness is quickly destroyed by cutting paper, hair, or plastic. An inexpensive pair of scissors for general household use might be described as essential quilting equipment, because it will spare your good shears for fabric.

Long, rustproof *pins* are desirable. Long pins will penetrate the dense layers of the quilt easily; rustproof pins prevent the possibility of nasty orange stains developing on long-term quilting projects. Rusty pin marks develop most noticeably in very damp climates, or on the work of a quilter who habitually holds pins in her mouth.

Ironing is an essential part of the patchwork sewing process. If possible, use a steam iron. Although I prefer to iron on a padded table, an ironing board will do. If you don't have a steam iron, spray the fabric lightly with a plant mister before you iron.

Although it's possible to make a quilt on your lap, a *big worktable* is helpful. If it's padded, you can iron on it, too. I put several layers of old blankets on top of my table, smoothed out every wrinkle, and stapled it tightly underneath the table. Then I stretched and stapled a heavy, closely woven canvas over the blanket. A table as long as the typical quilt, perhaps seven feet, is a great help, as the quilt can be spread flat on it.

Wash Fabric First?

Most quilt books will tell you to wash the fabric before you use it for patchwork, and this is sensible advice. I didn't follow it for many years, because I didn't have a washing machine and I did have huge quantities of small scraps. Surprisingly, I didn't have any resulting disasters, perhaps because I always washed and dried my quilts at cool temperatures only, or dry-cleaned them. But by following more expert advice and prewashing all fabric, you guarantee there won't be any disasters when you wash the quilt. Be sure to iron all fabric before marking or cutting.

An alternative to prewashing fab-ric is to dry-clean the quilt (may not be appropriate for cotton).

A lengthier discussion of fabrics and their attributes is found in the "Fabric and Color" chapter.

Marking and Cutting Triangles

There are three or four different ways to produce the triangles used so often in patchwork. Some methods are more precise than others; you can choose the one that suits you best. Always have one edge of the triangle parallel to the grain of the fabric.

Triangles Marked with Templates

Spread fabric out with the right side down, so that marking is done on the back of the fabric. Always iron fabric before marking. Lay the template on the edge of the cloth if it is straight, otherwise use a ruler to mark a straight line first. Use a fine-tip felt pen for marking around the template. (Test pen's waterfastness on a scrap of fabric.) Lay the second triangle upside down against the first, so they share a common cutting line (Photo 2-3).

2-3. *The second triangle shares a common cutting line.*

A great number of triangles can be marked before cutting. Putting the triangles right next to each other is the most economical use of the fabric.

Folding and Cutting Triangles From a Strip

Although less accurate, this method is a quick way to cut triangles. Start with a long strip of fabric, making sure that the edges are parallel and that the corners are good right angles.

1. Take the upper left corner of the strip and fold it down so that the end of the strip lines up with the bottom edge of the fabric, making a triangle. Iron the fold.
2. Cut along the right edge of the doubled triangle, separating it from the strip. The cut-off piece is actually a square folded diagonally (Photo 2-4).

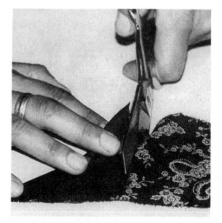

2-4. *Cut along right edge of doubled triangle. The cut-off piece is a square folded diagonally.*

3. Cut along the diagonal fold to make two triangles.
4. This process can be repeated down the length of the strip to produce a number of triangles (Photo 2-5).

2-5. *Repeat process down the length of strip to produce a number of triangles.*

The same principles of folding and cutting can be used to make the large triangles needed for the outer borders of a big quilt. Make sure the corners are square before you begin. If the strip of fabric is wider than your table, let it dangle over the edge, or lay it out on the floor (Photo 2-6).

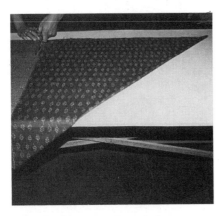

2-6. *Cut large triangles with the same method. You might want to cut these on the floor.*

Triangles from a Square

Two right triangles are formed whenever a square is divided diagonally. If you have a square template, this is an easy way to make triangles.

A carpenter's framing square or an L-shaped ruler can be used to make squares, which can then be cut diagonally to make triangles. The two edges of the fabric must be at ninety degrees to each other before you begin.

1. Position the legs of the L-shaped ruler so that each leg is measuring the same number of inches in from the two edges of the fabric. Mark the fabric along the edge of the ruler (Photo 2-7).

2-7. *Use an L-shaped ruler to mark squares. Mark at the same distance along the two edges of the fabric.*

2. By drawing a line diagonally across the square, triangles are formed (Photo 2-8).

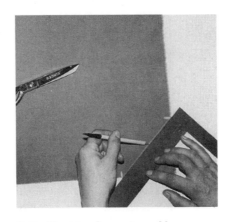

2-8. *Two triangles are formed by marking diagonally across the square.*

Cutting or Tearing Strips

Strips of fabric are used to make the borders that frame medallion patchwork. Don't forget to iron the fabric before measuring, marking, cutting, or tearing. Make all marks on the back side of the fabric. There are two ways to make accurate strips.

Mark and Cut Strips

Start along a straight edge of fabric. Measure and mark strips of the desired width, then trace along the edge of a yardstick (Photo 2-9).

2-9. *Strips can be cut after marking fabric.*

Clip and Rip Strips

It is just as accurate, and much quicker, to rip strips of fabric instead of cut them. Unfortunately, not all fabrics rip nicely. One-hundred-percent cotton rips cleanly, but blended cottons pucker, and synthetics often can't be ripped at all. Try it on a small piece of fabric first.

Make a small clip with the scissors at the edge of the fabric, then rip the fabric with a sharp, quick motion. Iron the strip afterward.

Ironing Tips

It pays to iron frequently, at every stage of the patchwork process. Don't try to cut pieces for patchwork out of un-ironed fabric, as they won't come out the right shape. Iron fabric before you measure, mark, or cut it. Using the iron after sewing each seam assures that you won't sew in any wrinkles or puckers.

Often, ironing can substitute for pinning, as the pieces of fabric will cling together by static electricity after they are ironed. Iron first, even if you are pinning as well.

I feel that it's best to iron the patchwork medallion symmetrically from the center, moving the iron outward on one side, then the other, then the two opposite sides.

Iron each seam after it is sewn, whether it is a seam that joins two small triangles together, or a seam that is six feet long. The seams are not ironed as in dressmaking, with the allowances on either side of the seam. Instead, ironing both allowances to one side of the seam adds strength to the quilt.

I don't iron seams from the backside of the quilt top. Instead, I iron on the right side, letting the seam allowances go to one side or the other at random.

Sewing Hints

Keep Your Sewing Machine in Good Condition

Don't keep sewing once you notice the tension is out of whack, the thread is tangling in big knots, or the machine is making peculiar shrieking or grating noises. Stop and try to figure out what is wrong. If you want your quilt and its many seams to last for a decade or two, then your sewing ma-

chine must operate at its best. The integrity of your quilt depends on the soundness of its patchwork seams.

An article in the February 1991 issue of *Threads*, "Why Stitches Skip and Fabric Puckers," by Gale G. Hazen, is well worth reading for its explanation of *how* a sewing machine works and what we can do to keep it working at its best.

Don't Oil Your Machine Unless You Have Cleaned out the Lint First

If you use your sewing machine a lot, it will need periodic oiling. But you will be creating rather than solving problems if you don't clean out the lint, fuzz, and bits of thread *before* you oil. Adding oil to the lint and debris will turn it into an oily, sticky glob that can really jam up your machine. I use a watercolor paintbrush to remove lint and a pair of tweezers to coax out tangled threads.

Adjust the Tension

Above my sewing table, I keep a diagram that explains tension, and I consult it whenever I get confused. The drawing first shows a balanced tension in cross section, with the two threads properly intertwined at the center of the fabric (Illustration 2-10).

With my machine, if the top thread is being carried to the bottom of the fabric at each stitch, and the bottom thread is lying quite visible on the undersurface of the fabric, it means there is "not enough" tension on the top thread, so it is loose and sloppy, or that there is "too much" tension on the bottom thread, so it has pulled the top thread down. I correct this situation by turning the top adjustment clockwise to get more tension on the top thread (Illustration 2-11).

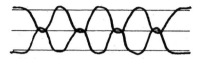

2-10. *The cross section shows balanced tension.*

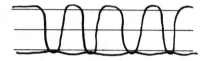

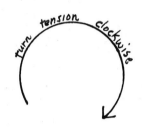

2-11. *If top thread is drawn underneath, turn knob clockwise to increase tension. (Check to see how your machine works.)*

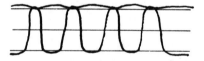

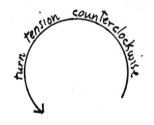

2-12. *If bottom thread is drawn to top, loosen tension by turning knob counterclockwise. (Your machine may work differently.)*

However, if the top thread is lying visible on the upper surface of the fabric, and the bottom thread has been drawn up to the top at each stitch, it means there is too much tension on the top thread, which is pulling the bottom thread too far upward. In this situa-

35

tion, I turn the tension counterclockwise (Illustration 2-12).

Consult your sewing machine manual for specific instructions related to your machine.

Make Quarter-inch Seams Without Marking First

Traditional patchwork instructions suggest that every piece of fabric be marked on all sides, one-fourth inch in from the cut edges. This insures precise quarter-inch seams and, of course, precise patchwork. But there are those of us who would have given up patchwork years ago if this were really necessary. If you like to sew quickly and are not of a meticulous nature, you probably won't want to mark seams before sewing them.

The modern "all-purpose" presser foot is a perfect guide for sewing quarter-inch seams, because it is exactly one-fourth inch from the needle to the outer edge of the foot. Just keep the edge of the presser foot and the edge of the fabric aligned while you sew.

Another way to avoid marking seams is to put a piece of tape on the throat plate of your machine, parallel to the direction of sewing, and one-fourth inch from the needle. Keep the edge of the tape and the edge of the fabric aligned as you sew.

Support Your Quilt

As the quilt top grows in size, it increases in weight and awkwardness. Allowing a big quilt top to hang down toward the floor as you sew can cause several problems. Instead of the seams being fed straight under the needle, they are pulled to the side, so that constant shiftings and adjustments are necessary. Sometimes the weight of the

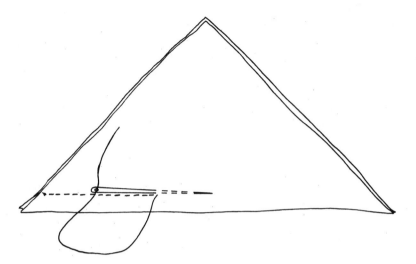

2-13. *Gather three or four stitches on the needle before pulling through.*

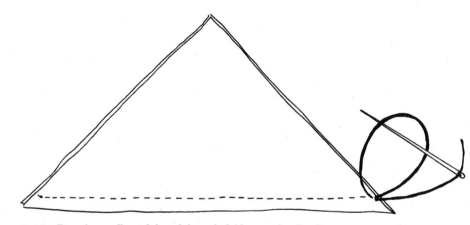

2-14. *Pass the needle and thread through the loop and pull tight.*

quilt top can strain the seams, or even bend the needle.

Position the sewing machine so it is at the right-hand side of the sewing table, leaving enough space to support the quilt top. If the table is too small for this, put a small table, bench, or chair next to it, to help support the quilt top.

Invest in Good Thread

Don't use cheap, old, or weak thread. An extra dollar spent buying good quality thread may ensure that your quilt is still in good condition when your grandchildren inherit it. I often use cotton quilting thread for machine sewing because it is strong, but I also use a cotton-wrapped polyester thread or a good polyester thread. For hand sewing, I would suggest good cotton thread only.

Machine Sewing

Set your machine for straight stitching, twelve stitches to the inch, and adjust the tension if necessary. Generally, it is not necessary to backstitch when doing patchwork, but you can if you want to.

If you are getting tiny snags in the fabric as you sew, perhaps the needle needs changing. The point may have developed a tiny barb that is catching the fabric. Sewing with a bent or damaged needle will eventually damage your machine.

Hand Sewing

Whether you make an entire quilt by hand, or only sew the occasional stitch, you will find hand sewing less frustrating if you use a good, strong, cotton thread. Do not choose a synthetic thread for hand sewing, as it will snarl.

Running Stitch

Patchwork pieces are usually sewn together using a single rather than a double thread, as it is thought that doubled threads will rub against each other and be weakened. Tie a knot in the end of the thread before you begin stitching. The running stitch used to sew patchwork by hand passes the needle and thread up and down through the fabric. Three or four stitches can be gathered on the needle before it is pulled through (Illustration 2-13).

To end a line of stitching, make a tailor's knot, as shown on page 36. First, take a small stitch and pull it part way through, leaving a loop.

Pass the needle and thread through the loop (Illustration 2-14).

Pull the knot tight.

When sewing by hand, I usually make a small knot every two or three inches. The stitching can continue after the knot because the thread is not cut. Then, if the thread breaks, the whole seam won't unravel. I do this periodic knotting on any long seams and also when I am hand sewing the binding.

To prevent tangles, cut short lengths of thread and run the thread against a piece of beeswax or candle. Try several types of needle to find what kind you prefer, but choose the smallest size you can thread easily.

It may feel awkward at first, but a thimble on the middle finger of your sewing hand will save your flesh and speed your sewing. See the chapter "Don't Quit Till It's Quilted" for further discussion of thimbles.

Fabric and Color

3

If you want an extraordinary quilt, don't use ordinary fabric. This doesn't mean you need expensive fabric, but you do need fabric with visual impact. Don't be timid in choosing fabric.

Attributes of Fabrics

Cottons

Cotton fabrics are traditional for quilts, and for good reason. They handle well and give a supple feel to the quilt. Besides the usual broadcloth and calico, you might use denim, corduroy, velveteen, or sailcloth. Cotton strips can usually be torn rather than cut, as cotton will rip cleanly and seldom puckers.

Blends

Cotton-synthetic blends seem to lack the depth of color found in 100-percent cottons and are harder to quilt. Blends do not usually rip well, because the edges pull and pucker. Although blends are not usually a quiltmaker's first choice, they are cheap, widely available, and fairly indestructible.

Rayon

Although a man-made fiber, rayon shares many of cotton's attributes and works well in patchwork.

Synthetics

I'm not fond of synthetics for patchwork. Aside from being untraditional for use in quilts, they are hard to work with, tending to slip or shift their position, and they do not accept the needle readily. I will sometimes overlook these defects if the unusual pattern or bright color of a synthetic fabric tempts me.

Stretchy Fabrics

Using stretchy fabrics for patchwork is seldom worth the bother, as they will not maintain their shape for precise cutting and sewing. I might choose a special stretchy fabric for its beauty, despite the possible frustration involved. Pin well, and baste if necessary. But stretchy fabrics can sometimes be used deliberately for exciting sculptural effects on borders that you intend to stuff underneath with extra batting.

Satin and Velvet

Satin, velvet, and other luxury fabrics are fussy to work with because they slide about while being sewn, but they give such a lush and spectacular effect that they seem worth the extra effort. Both children and adults take a tactile pleasure in these fabrics. Velvet

You have to go pretty haywire on fabric before it looks ugly.

—Coleen Vanderheide

has a nap that must be considered when cutting and laying out pieces. These fabrics are delicate, and may retain marks from pinning or from ripping out seams.

Silk

This ancient and beautiful fabric is luxurious and sensuous, with a wonderful texture and vibrant colors. Silk is somewhat fragile, and may wear out before the other fabrics in the quilt top. It is easily marred by pins or ripped out seams.

Wool

Once frequently used in quilt tops, this warm and cozy fabric is usually neglected today. The unusual depth of color in most wools makes them welcome additions to a quilt top, if their greater bulk can be handled.

Recycled Fabric

Used fabrics are the traditional stuff of quilts. Both for economy and sentiment, cutting up favorite old clothes makes sense. Be careful to avoid worn areas, shiny spots, or other flaws. A very fragile, old fabric may sometimes be used if another stronger fabric is placed underneath. Choose one of a similar color, because it will show through if the delicate top fabric rips or wears away.

Needlework

A quilt can become a showpiece for other kinds of handiwork. A delicate crocheted or knitted doily might star as the center of a medallion. Pieces of lace can be stitched to a dark background fabric and incorporated into the patchwork. Secondhand stores sometimes have beautifully embroidered garments that can be cut up for patch-

work. (See Plate 6, Ghislaine's Quilt, center.) Or you can do your own embroidery on the quilt. Delicate needlework should probably be carefully basted onto a background fabric, and removed at laundry time.

Combining Fabrics

The Grab Bag

There is a certain logic in using only one type of fabric in a quilt. Washing or cleaning will be more straightforward with a single fabric. A harmoniously coordinated quilt is perhaps more easily achieved by choosing fabric cautiously.

But I would not wish to relinquish the pleasures of the grab bag. For variety, for contrast, for surprise and drama, the greatest range of fabrics gives the most satisfaction. Almost any fabric may be used if thought is given to its attributes and qualities.

Thick and Thin Fabrics

When you sew a thick piece and a thin piece of fabric together, iron the seam so that the thicker fabric remains flat, with the seam allowance of the thinner fabric folded over it, as shown in Illustration 3-1.

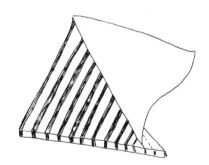

3-1. *Iron the seam so that the thicker fabric is flat, with the thinner fabric folded over it.*

Dark and Light Fabrics

The seam allowance of the darker fabric occasionally shows through the lighter fabric when the two are sewn together. Iron the seam so that the lighter fabric is flat, with the darker fabric's seam allowance folded over. Trim the darker seam allowance a little closer to the seam if necessary.

Wash First, or Dry-clean Forever

If you are willing to dry-clean the quilt, virtually all fabrics may be combined in a quilt top. If you want to be able to wash the quilt, then wash the fabrics first. Any fabric emerging unharmed from a hot wash and dry is safe to use in a quilt. Remember that dry-cleaning is not an environmentally friendly process.

Avoid Fraying and Unraveling

Fabrics that fray easily and could cause a seam to unravel should be cut with pinking shears if possible. Otherwise, zig-zag around each patchwork piece before it is sewn into the quilt top, or zig-zag the seam allowances of seams that have already been sewn.

Reinforce Delicate Fabrics

Very soft, delicate, or fragile fabrics should have a stronger piece of fabric in the same color range placed underneath them. This adds strength, and prevents the batting from showing through if the top fabric wears poorly. A fragile fabric can also be reinforced with a piece of thin white organza or other transparent fabric over the top to prevent wear.

Label It

If your choice of unusual fabrics creates a quilt that will need special care, this information should be written in indelible ink on a separate piece of plain fabric and attached to the back of the quilt as a label.

Bits and Pieces

Besides aesthetic choices, you must make practical choices based on the amounts of different fabrics you have. Two yards of a fabric will allow you to make design choices not possible if you have only a small snippet of that same fabric.

But tiny scraps are the traditional raw material of patchwork, and are certainly not detrimental from a design perspective. Treasured bits of fabric will be highlighted and featured in the central medallion, in narrow borders, or in small patchwork pieces. The center of the medallion is the visual focus of your quilt, and will probably start with a tiny, carefully hoarded scrap of beloved fabric.

Utilizing small pieces of treasured fabric is prudent and thrifty, and it also encourages creative solutions to design problems. A border built from small multicolored scraps will usually be more elaborate and elegant than a border made from a single, more abundant fabric.

Variety of fabric is much more important than the size of the pieces. A large supply of small scraps is going to yield a more interesting and creative quilt than a small supply of new yardage. Treasure your scraps, stockpile bits of fabric, purchase fabric you really like when you are able, and value what is on hand.

As the medallion gets bigger, the borders do too. When you get to the outside borders, you may need to buy a yard or two of fabric to complete the quilt top. You will probably be shopping for backing material as well. Be sure to save the scraps. You'll want them for your next quilt.

The Pleasures of Pattern

Small Prints and Calicoes

The dainty calicoes and tiny repetitive prints so often favored for patchwork are safe, but perhaps not too exciting. A quilt composed entirely of small prints will have a sedate, traditional look. Such a quilt may be calming, soothing, comforting; desirable attributes when you want to curl up and go to sleep. But if you want a quilt that makes you wake up and sing, perhaps some of the fabrics in it should be more lively. Small prints and calicoes can best be used as background, to contrast with fabrics of stronger and more emphatic pattern.

Large Motifs

Boldly printed floral designs, paisleys, abstract patterns, and batiks are great in quilts. Cutting patchwork pieces out of large-print fabric offers several design advantages.

Patchwork triangles and squares can be carefully laid out and cut so that

3-2. *Fabric is cut so that the motifs have dramatic focus.*

the fabric motifs are given dramatic focus (Illustration 3-2). Flowers or geometric forms can then be precisely positioned to emphasize and amplify the patchwork design (Illustration 3-3).

A very different effect, more subtle and haphazard, occurs when patchwork triangles are cut from large-print fabric without consideration of the printed design. A side-by-side layout of triangles during cutting will result in the fabric motifs being divided at random. Some triangles may show mostly background, while others may have the motif off-center or cut in two (Illustration 3-4).

This more accidental positioning of the fabric motif results in a softer, less emphatic, and often more visually intriguing patchwork design than if the fabric motif was precisely placed (Illustration 3-5).

Geometric Prints

Fascinating patterns develop when geometric prints are cut up and recombined in patchwork. The border of pointy triangles in Mama's Sunflower (See Plate 25) was made from a batik fabric with limitless design possibilities. Illustration 3-6 shows some other patterns that could emerge from this fabric.

Border Prints

Not surprisingly, border prints make great quilt borders. Start by cutting your border print yardage into its separate borders. This will give you a number of long strips of varied design, which can be used to frame and emphasize a medallion.

Cutting a border print into triangles for patchwork offers some interesting effects, as you can rotate and transpose the linear pattern of the fabric.

3-3. *Patchwork design is emphasized by the placement of the flowers and/or geometric shapes.*

3-4. *Some triangles show mostly background, while others have the motif off-center or cut in two.*

Plaids and Stripes

The geometric nature of plaids and stripes offers intriguing design potential. These fabrics are often thought of as staid and conventional, but they can produce startling and unusual effects when used in patchwork. Striped and plaid fabrics can be cut lengthwise, crosswise, or diagonally, each yielding very different effects. If the plaid or stripe is composed of numerous colors, particular colors will be emphasized depending on how the fabric is cut.

Texture

Fabric without pattern is important in patchwork to contrast and highlight patterned pieces. In a medallion quilt, the medallions are often made of patterned fabric framed by borders of plain fabric.

More subtle than pattern or color, the texture of fabric influences how a quilt looks and how it feels. Wool, velveteen, and corduroy absorb light to give depth, shading, and a soft, warm touch. Satins and glazed chintzes bring luster, shine, and light to a quilt. Velvets magically change hue as they both reflect and absorb light. Brocade fabrics offer small tactile pleasures with their subtle woven designs. Roughly furrowed corduroy, fuzzy chenille, and bumpy seersucker surprise the touch.

You would probably never choose quilt fabric solely on the basis of texture, but you would be equally foolish to ignore it altogether. Varied textures will embellish and enhance the patchwork design, giving added visual and tactile impact.

Theme Fabrics, Fabric Themes

Unusual fabrics can suggest a theme for a quilt. Fabrics printed with sailboats, butterflies, or dinosaurs could provoke unique theme quilts; handkerchiefs, scarves, and linen tea towels are sometimes printed with pictures that can be framed by medallions of patchwork.

Or the theme may be the fabrics themselves. A quilt could be made entirely of ribbons, batiks, or flour sacks. You could start a medallion with your daughter's first little dress, and add borders through the years sewn from her favorite garments. You could do the same thing with your husband's old plaid shirts. You could sew a permanent memento of a holiday with fabrics purchased on the trip. The sky's the limit.

Creating in Color

Working with color may worry you. You might feel that all the colors should go together, with nothing that clashes or contrasts too strongly. Although this is good wardrobe advice, it may result in a boring quilt.

I like bright colors. I like colors that clash, lots of different colors put together in a quilt, colors that knock your eyeballs out. My favorite patchwork is anything but timid in its hues. Your color aesthetic may be quite different than mine. You may like subtle gradations and muted blends of color, a harmonious shading of hues, a more delicate palette.

How do you choose colors for a quilt? Most simply, choose colors that you like. You must rely on your own preferences and your own instincts about what is pleasing to you. But be bold! Don't be afraid of color.

This Antique Crazy Square is undimmed by time, its maker's bright spirit still shining bold and clear (Plate 7, Antique Crazy Square). The pre-

3-5. *Accidental positioning of the fabric motif results in an intriguing patchwork design.*

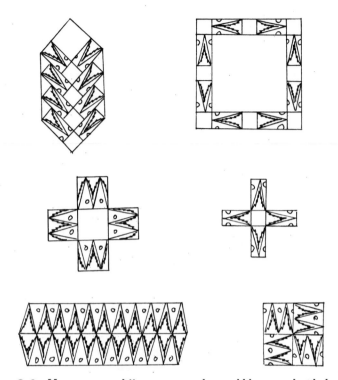

3-6. *Here are some different patterns that could be created with the fabric used in Mama's Sunflower (Plate XX).*

dominantly dark, rich colors glow more eloquently because of the contrasting lighter fabrics and the vivid colors of the fanciful embroidery stitches.

Monochromatic Hues

If you are hesitant, you may want to choose a single color as the main theme for your quilt. A monochromatic quilt might be composed of different printed fabrics with the same background color, containing every possible hue, tint, shade, or hint of that particular color.

A quilt of limited colors will gain variety and interest from different textures: thick wools or velvets that absorb light, shiny reflective satins, rough-woven hopsacking or corduroys. Single-color quilts are usually restful and tasteful, but sometimes lacking in zest. Adding small touches of contrasting color will liven up a monochromatic quilt.

Twilight Star is definitely a blue quilt, composed of varied blues, blue-grays, and blue-greens, but it is saved from boredom by generous dashes of an exultant red-orange (Plate 8, Twilight Star).

The red-orange leaves in the center triangle suggested later additions of the same bright hue. A red-orange and blue-green plaid surrounds the triangle. All the floral fabrics are blue in background but have touches of red or orange in their flowers. The warmer coloration is echoed in a plaid taffeta at the outer edges of the quilt. This is indeed a blue quilt, but the red-orange accents give it pizzazz.

Ember's Quilt is green, composed entirely of light and dark prints and solids (Plate 9, Ember's Quilt, center). The only contrasts come from the secondary colors used in the printing of the patterned fabric. Dusky cotton velveteen, shiny synthetic velvet, and a shimmering, sensuous silk velvet provide subtle contrast and variety.

Clashing Colors

The opposite of a monochrome is using colors for their shock value, pitting one against the other in eye-boggling clashes. The Guatemalans and the Amish are experts at manipulating color.

These are colors that fight each other, that vibrate at their boundaries, that stretch your visual tolerance to its limit. These are the colors your mother told you not to put together; like anything forbidden, they are exciting. Clashing colors thrill and electrify. I love clashing, clanging, brilliantly discordant colors; but not everybody does.

For the Klemtu Sunrise wall hanging, I picked my brightest fabrics and colors and set them against each other in violent contrast (Plate 10, Klemtu Sunrise). I was striving for that vibrant afterimage that appears on closed eyelids after gazing at a brilliant image. Luminously transposed colors, strong contrasts between bright dazzling silks and intensely shadowed velvets, and flamelike triangles of yellow create a patchwork that can't be overlooked.

The clashes in Rheannon's Quilt (Plate 11, Rheannon's Quilt, detail) and Andy's Quilt (Plate 12, Andy's Quilt) are more subtle; the colors are exuberant but not alarming. The bright and cheerful fabrics do not clash unrelentingly, yet they go beyond the classic harmonies.

Contrasting Colors

Monochromatic quilts run the risk of being boring or insipid. Terrifically clashing quilts threaten insomnia. Contrasting colors are a happy compromise.

I enjoy the generous use of contrasting colors and will usually let three or four colors interact in a quilt, with touches of other colors as well. Even where one color predominates, I add small doses of many other colors for contrast and accent.

Adding neutral colors to a quilt is always a safe bet, allowing the more exotic colors a chance to shine in contrast. Black or white, unbleached muslin, tan, beige, gray, and cream are all effective contrasts to brighter or bolder colors.

An Antique Roman Stripe quilt has randomly placed dark bands within each square that contrast with the lighter tones of beige and cream (Plate 13, Antique Roman Stripe). The red zig-zags contrast both in color and placement.

Ghislaine's Quilt uses light-colored fabrics to emphasize the design (Plate 14, Ghislaine's Quilt). A rich white brocade enhances the antique embroidered bands in the center of the quilt; very pale pink triangles contrast agreeably with darker hues and form a sawtooth border.

Merging Colors

Colors can be softened and blended, or heightened and intensified, by intermingling their near neighbors on the color wheel.

The Desire's Inferno quilt is most definitely a red quilt (Plate 15, Desire's Inferno, detail). But when you look closely at the stripes that compose it, you will see all the neighboring hues of red: orange, pink, maroon, scarlet, magenta, purple, and brown. The closeness of the colors to the predominating red merges the whole quilt into a vibrant hue that seems redder than red.

The Mystery of Life crazy quilt has a yellow sun composed of many warm hues, some only distant relations to the dominant yellow (Plate 16, Mystery of Life). Brown, pink, orange, and gold combine to stretch the definition of a "yellow" quilt.

Echoing Colors

If there is a painting or photograph you are especially fond of, it might be an interesting exercise to make a quilt that echoes the colors of the picture. If the colors in the picture are beautiful, the colors in your quilt will be too.

Put in every single color, even if it appears only in very small amounts in the picture, and even (or especially) if it contrasts strongly with the other colors. These small touches of high contrast give life and drama to your quilt.

You can also echo the colors of a favorite fabric. If you choose an exciting printed fabric to begin the center medallion, you may decide to echo its colors in later borders. Again, it will be more successful if you use every single color in the print.

Byzantium's color theme is first stated in a small paisley-patterned black triangle, joined to a red Hawaiian floral etched in gold (Plate 17, Byzantium). Red and black dominate this quilt, which has gold highlights; but the touches of blue in the paisley fabric are echoed as well. Tiny specks of pink and green in the paisley are echoed in the floral motifs of the outer black border.

Conversely, if you have a large amount of patterned fabric, you might use it abundantly in large borders and echo its colors in small patchwork details. The Midnight quilt echoes the multicolored speckles of the black fabric in the vivid accenting borders (Plate 18, Midnight).

Rainbow Spectrum

Colors following each other in rainbow progression are always beautiful (Plate 19, Susan's Rainbow). Adjoining rainbow colors may clash, but the overall effect is one of harmonious contrast. Utilizing the multitude of hues within each color will give richness and depth.

Colors for Others

Choosing colors for a quilt to be made for someone else is a special challenge. A peek in his or her closet may give you clues to favorite colors, or matching someone's bedroom wallpaper and curtains may be appropriate. But don't pick colors you hate yourself. After all, you'll be working with them for months.

The colors of Mama's Medallion were easy to choose, because my mother has always surrounded herself with rich pinks and moss greens (Plate 20,

Mama's Medallion). I flashed back to the kitchen wallpaper of my childhood when I saw the green-and-pink fabric that became the top and bottom borders. The pink chintz brought to mind not only my mother but also my great-aunt, whose color preferences she shared. The hot pink and purple are my favorite colors, and perhaps remind my mother of me.

When making quilts for friends or customers, I find it most satisfactory if they pick out the fabric. But even if they want to buy new fabric, I ask them to pick out some fabric from my supply as well. This adds variety and makes it more likely that I will enjoy working with the colors they have chosen.

The Laws of Color

There are both scientific and aesthetic laws of color. Color wheels and color charts present color in a systematic and rational fashion. Whether you aim to harmonize, blend, or clash, a little knowledge about the characteristics and interactions of colors will help. Browse your library for books on color theory, color mixing, and color laws. Consult art books and fashion magazines for helpful explanations and examples of color.

Symbolism and Sentiment

Colors are rich in symbolism. You can pick colors to convey a mes-

sage or emphasize a theme. In the Western world, white traditionally signifies purity, red denotes courage, black expresses grief. These are cultural symbols, but you may have your own color symbolism that speaks to you more eloquently.

Although the colors you choose might unconsciously mirror your feelings, you can also use color more deliberately to express an emotion or evoke a mood. Your private, emotional responses to color can overlay your quilt with added significance and meaning. Certain colors are understood culturally to express certain emotions, but only you can choose the colors that best express your own feelings.

Color Is Free — Use It!

In the Middle Ages, sumptuary laws forbade commoners from using certain colors. Through much of history, because of their rare ingredients or difficult manufacture, particular colors were too expensive to be commonly used.

In contrast, the modern world is blessed with a wonderful array of available colors. Glowing colors, rare tints, and rich deep hues are no longer more costly than drab and ordinary shades. Color is now free, and we are free to use it lavishly and with joy.

How a Quilt
Is Built

There are millions of quilts and many ways to make them. I'd like to introduce you to my method for making patchwork medallion quilts by showing step by step how Nancy's Quilt came into being. Once you have mastered the basic concepts of using triangles or strips to form the concentric borders, you can vary the possibilities infinitely to create your own original designs.

Don't try to copy Nancy's Quilt. Instead, study the techniques and blend them with your own ideas, preferences, and creative inspiration to make a special quilt of your own.

Getting Ready

Start with fabric you already have; pieces both big and small are needed. Gather a pile of fabric that you like, and don't worry whether the fabrics match or go together. Bold patterns and colors add life and interest to your patchwork design.

You will probably have a few square inches of some fabrics and a yard or two of others. Don't rush out and buy a lot of fabric at this point. As the quilt gets bigger you may want to choose more. It's wise to wash and iron all fabric before you start cutting. See the "Fabric and Color" chapter for more discussion of fabric and its attributes.

Nancy chose bright, clear colors, for her quilt, with a few neutral tones for contrast. She selected several border prints, which provided various strong motifs. She also chose several other bold prints, a few small calicoes and flower prints, a bit of black velvet, a big piece of blue broadcloth, and an orange-red cotton of extraordinary intensity.

Medallion Patchwork

Let's start with a brief lesson in making a patchwork medallion. More detailed instructions will follow as we begin to make the quilt top.

When you are making medallion patchwork, you don't need to design first. Rather than copying a pattern or drawing your design on paper ahead of time, you simply make a number of small decisions as your quilt progresses.

A medallion quilt starts in the center with a small square of fabric. Four triangles will be sewn around it to form the first border. Four strips will be added to create the second border. The fabric for each border can be chosen as you come to it.

I think we can safely dispense with the notion that the quilt-maker's brains are in her needle.

—Beth Gutcheon
The Perfect Patch-work Primer

49

1. Begin with a square, and sew on two triangles to opposite sides (Illustration 4-1).

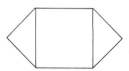

4-1. *Sew two triangles to opposite sides of a square.*

2. Sew on two more triangles to the remaining two sides of the square (Illustration 4-2).

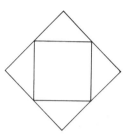

4-2. *Sew two triangles to the remaining sides of the square, so that triangles surround all four sides.*

3. Sew two strips to opposite sides of the square (Illustration 4-3).

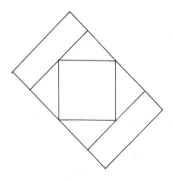

4-3. *Sew two strips of fabric to opposite sides of the square.*

4. Sew two longer strips to the other two sides (Illustration 4-4).

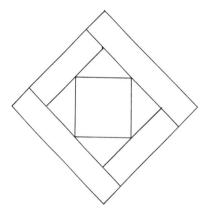

4-4. *Sew two longer strips to the other two sides of the square.*

5. Sew on another set of four larger triangles (Illustration 4-5).

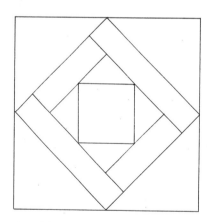

4-5. *Add four larger triangles.*

6. Sew on another set of four strips (Illustration 4-6).

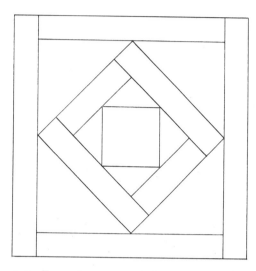

4-6. *Frame the square with four more strips.*

The medallion quilt top will grow bigger and bigger as more borders are added. The order of triangles and strips can be varied, as well as the dimensions of the borders. Later we will see how to make more complicated patchwork borders and how to develop a more elaborate design.

Making Nancy's Quilt

I use the word *border* quite loosely here and in the next section. The sixth and seventh borders don't encircle the quilt completely. In a more correct sense, what I've labeled as the fourth, fifth, and sixth borders are actually different segments of a single complex border. But we will call each a separate border, in order to explain its construction more easily. Each is a separate border in my mind, because each involved a different set of decisions, and each is constructed of four units attached to the four sides of the medallion.

Medallion is a funny word too, because it keeps growing and changing just like the quilt we are making. Because of the concentric nature of a medallion quilt, each time a border is added, the definition of the medallion changes to include it. Each new border changes the dimensions of the medallion. At some vague point, we may begin to call the medallion a quilt top instead.

The First Border

I chose a deep-hued floral square for the center of the medallion and surrounded it with a subdued border of gray-blue triangles.

Lay the first triangle along one edge of the square, lining it up so that a little "ear" pokes out on either side (Photo 4-7). Right sides of the fabrics are facing each other. Iron the two pieces so that they stick together by static electricity, or pin them together.

Sew together with a quarter-inch seam. The modern presser foot measures one-fourth-inch from the needle to the outside edge of the foot, and can be used to maintain a quarter-inch

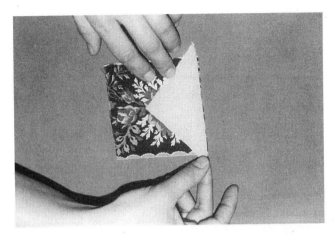

4-7. *Center the first triangle along the edge of the square. Little "ears" will stick out from either side.*

4-8. *Use the edge of the presser foot as a guide for sewing quarter-inch seams.*

4-9. *After pressing the seam of the first triangle, place the second triangle opposite it. Little ears will extend on either side of the square.*

51

seam by keeping the edge of the foot running right alongside the edge of your fabric (Photo 4-8). Sew slowly if you have trouble keeping the seam straight.

Press the seam allowance flat, from the front of the fabric. Throughout the entire quiltmaking process, you will want to iron each seam right after it is sewn, so that the quilt top stays flat and smooth.

On the opposite side of the square, place the second triangle, with little ears extending out on either side (Photo 4-9).

Press the seam open, ironing from the front of the fabric.

The same process is followed for the third triangle (Photo 4-10). Again, the little ears stick out on either side.

Three sides of the border have been sewn on and pressed open.

Adding the fourth triangle returns the medallion to a square (Photo 4-11). The little ears can be cut off or left, as they will be covered up when the next border is sewn on.

How Big Should the Triangles Be?

Measurements don't need to be terribly precise. If the long side of the triangle is about one-half-inch longer than the side of the square, the seam allowance will take up the extra amount and create a good fit (Illustration 4-12).

If you are a perfectionist, you'll probably take a great deal of care in measuring exactly to get a precise fit. If you don't care too much about being perfect, you'll find it much easier, and just as satisfying, to take a good guess and use whatever triangles seem to fit. It's a lot less bother, and the results will still be pleasing.

Larger triangles: Using larger triangles will give a broader border.

4-10. *Center the third triangle so that the ears overlap the other two triangles.*

4-11. *The fourth triangle brings the medallion to a square.*

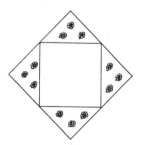

4-12. *For a good fit, make the base of each triangle about one-half inch longer than the square.*

When you sew on the first two triangles, do just as before, positioning them so that an equal amount sticks out on either side. These ears are a lot bigger now, of course, but will be handled the same way (Illustration 4-13). The seam will be sewn the length of the side of the square, and then pressed open.

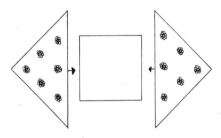

4-13. *Larger triangles will create a broader border.*

Line up the third triangle with the third edge of the square, again positioning it so an equal amount sticks out on either side (Illustration 4-14). The seam goes beyond the square on either side. After the seam is sewn, the ears are clipped off, and the seam is pressed open.

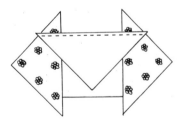

4-14. *Line up the third triangle with the third edge of the square, so that equal amounts overlap on two sides.*

The fourth triangle is sewn on in the same manner (Illustration 4-15). This makes a square with a broad border.

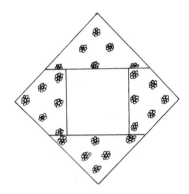

4-15. *Use the same method to add the fourth triangle.*

Smaller triangles: Quite a different effect is made by a border of triangles whose long edge is shorter than the side of the square.

Center each triangle on a side of the square, sew the seam, and press open (Illustration 4-16). You will notice that the triangles don't reach all the way to the corners of the square.

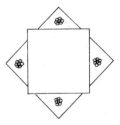

4-16. *After centering each triangle on a side of the square, sew the seam and press open. The triangles won't reach all the way to the corners of the square.*

When the next border is added, the corners of the inner square will be cut off, creating an octagon instead of a square in the center (Illustration 4-17). As you can see, the four triangles are now isolated from each other, rather than touching.

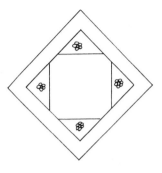

4-17. *Adding the next border changes the inner square to an octagon.*

There is no right or wrong size; deciding the size of the triangles is up to you, depending on the effect you want and the amount of fabric you have to work with.

4-18. *Here two triangles have been sewn to opposite sides of the square, and the seams have been pressed open.*

4-19. *Adding two more triangles makes a larger square. Tilt the square forty-five degrees for a diamond orientation.*

The Second Border

Triangles are again sewn onto opposite sides of the square. The triangles for this border were cut from a strongly patterned geometric border print. The black line was part of the border print fabric and will create a frame for the inner medallion.

Two triangles have been sewn on and the seams pressed open (Photo 4-18). Remember to iron each seam after sewing it.

A new and larger square is created with the addition of the other two triangles. The square is tilted forty-five degrees to a diamond orientation (Photo 4-19).

The Third Border

I chose black velvet for the next border, as a way of focusing attention on the inner medallion and providing a visual pause before the more complicated patchwork to follow.

Strips of fabric composing this border can be marked and cut, or sometimes they can be ripped instead. It is easiest to work with long strips, cutting off the extra length after the strip is sewn to the square.

Lay the strip along the edge of the square, with right sides together. As you can see, the edge of the previous border was somewhat uneven. To deal with this, bring the strip in to line up with the edge of the skimpier triangle, giving a quarter-inch seam here (Photo 4-20). This will create a broader seam allowance along the bigger triangle. The excess seam allowance can be trimmed off after the seam is sewn. Seams narrower than one-fourth-inch

4-20. *Strips of fabric form the next border. If the edge of the square is uneven, bring in the strip a little more.*

4-21. *Iron the seam open. Trim off any extra material if the fabric strip is longer than the medallion.*

4-22. *Four fabric strips now frame the growing medallion. Remember to iron each seam as you sew.*

4-23. *Contrasting triangles are sewn into two-triangle squares. Then the squares are sewn into strips.*

may fray and unravel, so take care here.

Sew the first and second strips onto opposite sides of the square.

Iron the seams open. If the strip is longer than the medallion, trim any extra length (Photo 4-21).

The third and fourth strips must be longer than the first two, because they extend over the ends of the two side strips.

Four strips now frame the growing medallion. Don't forget to iron all seams open (Photo 4-22).

The Fourth Border

The next border is again made with strips, but these are fancy patchwork strips composed of many small triangles. Two contrasting triangles are first sewn into two-triangle squares. The squares are then sewn into strips (Illustration 4-23).

I chose a green fabric with little squiggles for one set of triangles and a bright pink fabric for the other. Although I chose only two fabrics for the triangles, a greater variety could be used. The triangles are marked and cut

as described in the "Tools and Techniques" chapter.

Two contrasting triangles are sewn together along their long edges, with a quarter-inch seam allowance. After each two-triangle square is made, it is ironed open. The little ears that stick out can be clipped off or left.

Once you have decided how they are to be arranged, the two-triangle squares are sewn into strips. Try to match the points carefully (Photo 4-24).

The patchwork strip is sewn on in

4-24. *After determining your arrangement, sew the two-part squares into strips. Match points carefully.*

4-25. *Two patchwork strips, each made of four two-part squares, have been sewn on and ironed.*

the same way as the plain strip in the third border. Lay the patchwork strip along the edge of the medallion, with the right sides of the fabric facing each other. Pin the strip to hold it in place while you sew the seam.

The first two patchwork strips are sewn to opposite sides of the medallion and pressed open (Photo 4-25). Each strip is made of four two-triangle squares.

The remaining strips will have to be longer than the first two. I cut four plain squares to add at each end of the patchwork strips to lengthen them. Iron the strips open after you sew them on.

When you are matching up the corners, it pays to be careful, because this is where it will be the most noticeable if the seams don't meet exactly. Align the seams by putting a pin through the two seams to match them precisely (Photo 4-26).

The four patchwork strips enhance the medallion, framing it with a star (Photo 4-27).

Fancy Patchwork Patterns

It is interesting to take the two-triangle squares and use them to lay out a number of patterns around the inner medallion. Different designs result from orienting the squares in different ways. Illustration 4-28 shows a few of the possible choices and variations.

Number and size of triangles affects proportions: The proportions and the effect of the patchwork border will vary depending on the number and size of the triangles used to make it, as can be seen in Illustration 4-29.

Puzzling questions for many beginning quiltmakers are how many triangles do you need, and how big should they be? The answers depend on how precise you like to be. I usually

4-26. *Match corner seams carefully by putting a pin through the seams to align them properly.*

4-27. *The four patchwork strips frame the medallion with a star.*

make a guess and fudge a little if I'm wrong, but you may prefer to measure and calculate. If so, measure one side of the medallion to which you will be adding the patchwork border. Decide how many two-triangle squares are needed, and their exact size. Add quarter-inch seams to *each* side of *each* triangle. If, on the other hand, you prefer to guess instead of measure, you'll

probably make up a number of two-triangle squares and lay them out around your medallion, hopefully remembering that the squares will become smaller when sewn into strips, because of the quarter-inch seam allowance on each side. Then sew the squares into strips, and lay them around the medallion.

4-28. *Don't feel pinned in! You have many design choices.*

4-29. *Number and size of the triangles will determine the patchwork border.*

If the strips are too short, add more two-triangle squares. If they are just a little bit too short, trim some fabric off the four sides of the medallion (Illustration 4-30).

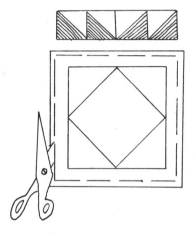

4-30. *Trim some fabric off the four sides of the medallion if the strips are only a little short.*

If the patchwork strips are too long, make the inner medallion a little bigger by framing it with another border of strips (Illustration 4-31).

4-31. *Frame the inner medallion with another border of fabric strips if the patchwork strips are too long.*

Another way of dealing with patchwork strips that are a little too short or a little too long is to adjust the seams. If too short, rip out a few seams between the squares and resew with a slightly narrower seam allowance.

A patchwork border that is too long can be shortened by resewing the seam allowances a tiny bit wider. Don't take out the first seam; just sew next to it.

You can make slight changes in the length of the patchwork strip by gently stretching to lengthen it; or you can shrink it a bit by dampening the strip and laying it out a little loosely, then ironing it with a steam iron.

The Fifth Border

A border print guarantees an exciting border. I chose a blue-flowered border print with bright yellow scallops for the next border. The strip of fabric is shown here upside down, with the right side of the fabric facing the right side of the medallion (Photo 4-32). The seam is being pinned before being sewn.

4-32. *Place border fabric upside down with right side in, and pin to the square.*

Two strips have been sewn on and ironed (Photo 4-33).

The remaining two strips need to be longer. Plain triangles are attached to the ends of the strips to lengthen them.

4-33. *Here two strips have been sewn on and ironed open.*

58

4-34. *Triangles sewn on at corners to lengthen the third and fourth strips must meet exactly at corner seams.*

4-35. *Small corner triangles change the medallion from a square to an octagon.*

For the triangles to fit accurately at the corners, cut the fabric strip a little big. Attach one triangle, position the strip right next to the medallion, and measure where the second triangle should be placed. The triangle will be sewn onto the strip with a quarter-inch seam, and you will want this seam to match up exactly with the seam above it, where the left-hand finger is pointing (Photo 4-34).

The medallion is changed from a square to an octagon with the addition of small triangles at the corners of the border strips (Photo 4-35).

Illustration 4-36 highlights other ways that the same border print fabric could have been used to frame the medallion.

Pinning the medallion to the wall lets you see clearly what you are creating. Leave it on the wall to enjoy while you begin to envision what you want to sew on next.

If you are wondering what the back of the patchwork medallion looks like, turn it over. It probably seems messy compared to the front, but that doesn't matter as long as all the seams are sound. If you find any poorly sewn seams that might unravel or come loose, now is the time to mend them.

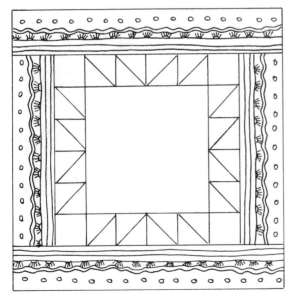

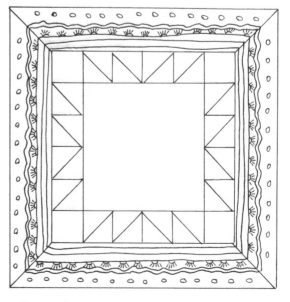

4-36. *Here are some other ways the border print fabric might have been used.*

4-37. *Lay triangles in place before sewing, to make sure correct edges are joined.*

4-38. *Align the opposing short sides of the triangles. Offset the triangles by seam width, leaving little ears. Then sew seam.*

The Sixth Border

Choosing a fabric with big, bold, stylized flowers, I carefully positioned the template so that the fabric motif was centered in the middle of the triangle. The plain triangles are vivid reddish orange. Like the fourth border, this one is made of small triangles, but they are sewn together in a different way.

Begin by laying the line of triangles in position before sewing them together, so you will know which edges are to be joined (Photo 4-37).

The triangles are laid on top of each other with opposing short sides aligned (Photo 4-38). Be sure to position the triangles off-center of each other by the width of the seam allowance, leaving the little ear from one triangle on one end of the seam and the little ear from the other triangle on the other end of the seam. If they are not offset in this way, the triangles won't match up after being sewn together. This is a difficult placement to make; don't be surprised if you occasionally have to rip out a seam and try again.

Sew the two triangles together along their short edges, then iron the seam open.

When you add the next triangle, it may be harder to judge its placement where it intersects with the previous seam. Just be sure to leave the little ear sticking out at the top. Because it has been affected by the seam, the little ear may be missing at the bottom (Photo 4-39).

The three-triangle trapezoid is shown here upside down and pinned in place, ready to be sewn onto the medallion (Photo 4-40).

After the seam is ironed, a larger trapezoid can be seen, made by the joining of the three-triangle trapezoid

4-39. *Placement of the next triangle is harder to judge, because the little ear is missing at the bottom.*

4-40. *A three-triangle patchwork unit is laid in place along edge of border print.*

4-41. *A larger trapezoid is created when the three-triangle unit is joined to the border print.*

4-42. *The four trapezoids enlarge the octagon. Plain triangles point to the center.*

to the border print (Photo 4-41).

The four trapezoidal units have enlarged the octagonal medallion. The four plain red-orange triangles draw attention to the center of the quilt top (Photo 4-42).

Again, I pin the medallion to the wall to get a proper look at it.

The Seventh Border

The medallion returns to a square when triangles with fabric strips at their bases are attached to the long sides of the octagon.

The first strip, of a diamond-printed fabric, is positioned with right sides together, along the base of the triangle (Illustration 4-43). The ends of the strip must extend well beyond the corners of the triangle.

The first strip has been sewn on and ironed open, and the next strip is about to be added. This second strip, of the same brilliant red-orange color as the triangles in the sixth border, also extends beyond the edges of the first strip (Illustration 4-44).

After the strips are sewn on and ironed, they will be trimmed at the same angle as the original triangle. Use a fine-tip felt pin and a straightedge to mark before cutting (Photo 4-45).

In Photo 4-46 I'm pointing to an irregularity in the edge of the underlying medallion. This unevenness is common, and of little concern, as long as the new unit is brought in a bit, so that the quarter-inch seam is maintained. The seam will be wider than one-fourth inch in places, which is fine; but it should never be less than that.

The medallion becomes six-sided briefly when the first two triangles have been added to either end (Photo 4-47).

Using a padded table instead of

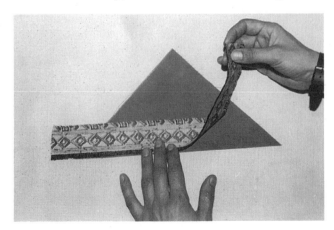

4-43. *Position the first strip along the base of the triangle, with ends extending well beyond corners of the triangle.*

4-44. *After the first strip is sewn on and ironed, add the second strip, which also extends beyond the corners.*

4-45. *Trim the strips at the same angle as the triangle, using a fine-tip felt pen and a ruler to mark before cutting.*

4-46. *Because the edge of the medallion is often uneven, bring in the new unit a bit to keep the quarter-inch seam.*

an ironing board makes ironing much easier as the medallion gets bigger and bigger.

When all four corner triangles have been attached, the medallion again becomes a square (Photo 4-48).

This time, when I hung the medallion on the wall, I tilted it forty-five degrees to see how it would look as a diamond.

The middle of Nancy's Quilt (Plate 21, Nancy's Quilt, center) shows how colors and shapes of varied borders interact to form a complex central image.

The Eighth Border

Narrow strips of a border-printed fabric are sewn to the four sides of the patchwork medallion, which now measures three feet square (Photo 4-49).

As the medallion grows, it becomes more awkward to handle. Keep the bulk of the fabric to the left of the sewing machine, rather than trying to force it through the narrow gap between the needle and the sewing machine arm. If you don't have a big worktable, perhaps the ironing board or a card table can be positioned next to your sewing machine to take some of the weight of the quilt top.

The Ninth Border

As the medallion or quilt top grows bigger, you may find it harder to choose fabric for it. Pin a possible fabric to the wall and place the medallion on top of it to get an idea of the effect. You will sometimes try several choices before you find the one you prefer. I chose this fabric for the wide outer border because its repetitive pattern was livelier than most small prints. Its blue background matched the blue

4-47. *With triangles sewn to two sides only, the medallion becomes a hexagon.*

4-48. *Now the medallion is once again square-shaped.*

4-49. *Narrow strips of border-printed fabric frame the three-foot-square medallion.*

4-50. *Center the first large triangle and pin with the right sides together. The ears sticking out will be large.*

triangles in the seventh border, and the black, red, yellow, and blue used in the print echoed colors already in the quilt.

The large triangles were cut out using the fold-and-cut method described in the "Tools and Techniques" chapter. Lay the strip out, then take hold of one corner and fold diagonally, so that the end of the strip is lined up with the adjacent long edge.

Iron the diagonal fold. Cut the triangles free of the strip, then cut the diagonal fold to make two triangles. Repeat the whole process to get two more triangles.

Center the triangle along the edge of the medallion, and pin in place (Photo 4-50). As always, the right sides of the fabric face each other. Because this border will be quite broad, the ears sticking out are large.

Two large triangles have already been sewn to two sides of the medallion, with a third triangle being added now. From now on, it may be easier to work on the floor. It won't hurt the quilt top to be stepped on with stockinged feet.

With all four triangles added, a broad border surrounds the inner medallion (Photo 4-51).

The Tenth Border

The quilt is shown back on the wall, with the tenth border already added (Photo 4-52). This border is actually three sets of narrow fabric strips, adding three concentric frames of red, yellow, and green.

A clean rug serves as a handy ironing board.

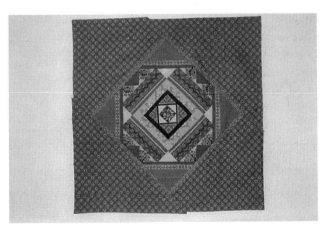

4-51. *When all four triangles are added, a broad border surrounds the inner medallion.*

4-52. *The next border is three concentric bands of narrow strips.*

4-53. *With the square tilted to a diamond, the quiltmaker stretches her imagination and herself to plan the final borders.*

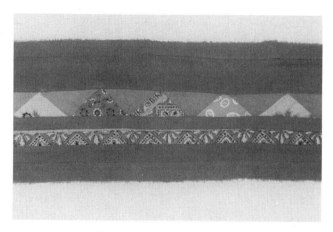

4-54. *Patchwork bands are sewn together first, then layered between fabric strips.*

4-55. *A final narrow border completes the medallion quilt top.*

The Eleventh Border

Back at the wall again, I plan the final borders. Circling all four sides of the quilt is plain blue broadcloth, chosen to highlight the inner medallion without strong contrast. I had already begun construction of the top border and pinned up everything to see how it looked before I sewed it together (Photo 4-53).

Top and Bottom Borders

Long bands of triangles are sewn together to crown the top and bottom borders.

I cut triangles from the many prints used in the quilt and alternated them with plain blue triangles. Sewn together in the same way as the triangles in the sixth border, the triangles are laid in position before they are sewn, to make sure they will be sewn together in the proper sequence.

These bands are layered between strips of green, red, and patterned fabric (Photo 4-54).

With a final narrow red border, the medallion quilt top is finished (Photo 4-55; Plate 22)! Quilting it will be the next step.

The chapter "Don't Quit Till It's Quilted" describes how this quilt was quilted.

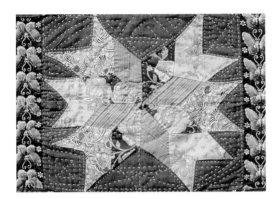

Plate 1. *However imperfect, my first attempt at quiltmaking, as represented by this detail of Yellow Butterfly, was thrilling.*

Plate 2. *In the creative process, even mistakes can be beautiful, as seen in Yellow Butterfly.*

Plate 3. *The central panel and the two end panels of Afternoon in Paradise are different, yet related.*

Plate 4. *The stylized flowers in the bottom medallion of Afternoon in Paradise deserved to be the center of attention.*

Plate 5. *A blue-and-white dot-and-dash border outlines the inner medallion of Afternoon in Pardise, while neutral beige corduroy contrasts with the varied patterns.*

Plate 6. *Pieces of a treasured dress enhance the center of Ghislaine's medallion quilt. (Quilt by Ghislaine de St. Venant.)*

Plate 7. *Dark, glowing shades are lit by brighter hues and bold embroidery in Antique Crazy Square.*

Plate 8. *Red-orange plaids and florals enliven the blue textures and patterns in Twilight Star.*

Plate 9. *Different shades of green combine with velvet textures and minimal color contrasts in the center of Ember's Quilt.*

Plate 10. *The classic sequence of the spectrum in the Klemtu Sunrise wall hanging controls its vivid colors.*

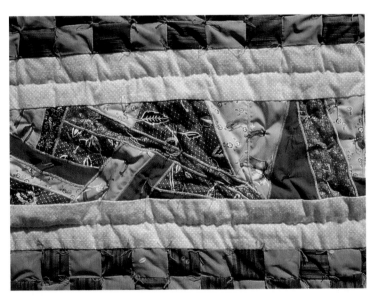

Plate 11. *Softly clashing colors are a welcome contrast for an infant's quilt, as seen in this detail of Rheannon's Quilt. (Quilt by Digby Island Quilters and friends.)*

Plate 12. *The colors and patterns in Andy's Quilt will not be ignored!*

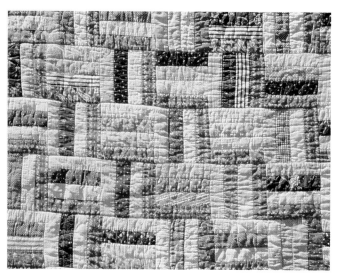

Plate 13. *The contrasting red zig-zag delineates the design amid random contrasts of dark and light in Antique Roman Stripe.*

Plate 14. *Ghislaine's Quilt combines white brocade and pink sawtooth. (Quilt by Ghislaine de St. Venant.)*

Plate 15. *This detail of Desire's Inferno shows how related hues enhance its warm red.*

Plate 16. *Bits of pink, brown, and gold spice up this yellow crazy quilt called Mystery of Life.*

Plate 17. *Various fabrics echo the red, black, gold, blue, pink, and green found in Byzantium's central paisley triangle.*

Plate 18. *Stripes and borders echo the colors sprinkled on the black background fabric in Midnight.*

Plate 19. *Classic rainbow hues radiate outward, while white diamonds provide contrast and focus for Susan's Rainbow.*

Plate 20. *Mama's Medallion incorporates the recipient's favorite colors.*

Plate 21. *The center medallion of Nancy's Quilt started with a square. A border of four triangles was added, and then another. A border of fabric strips frames the design.*

Plate 22. *Nancy's Quilt showcases a complex central image.*

Plate 23. *The design sequence for Sweet Baby Jane shows its development.*

Plate 24. *Far from being one-dimensional, patchwork can transform from one shape to another, as evidenced by these varied examples.*

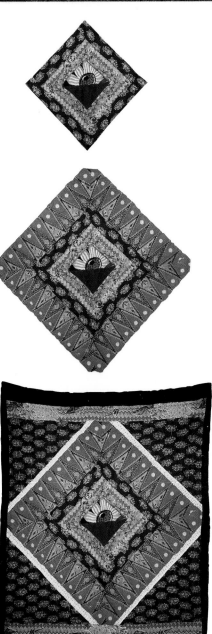

Plate 25. *The design sequence for Mama's Sunflower illustrates how one small sunflower can grow into a quilt.*

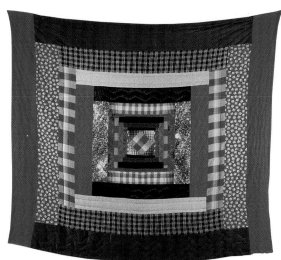

Plate 26. *The various stages of Stairway's design sequence build on one another.*

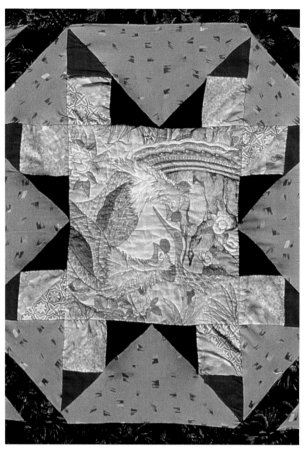

Plate 27. *Exotic birds are framed by a patchwork star in the middle of Bird Star, and then bordered by a black hexagonal square.*

Plate 28. *The outer star and black borders are an enlarged and enhanced version of Bird Star's inner medallion.*

Plate 29. *In Scarlet and Violet, strips of fabric are echoed in three succeeding borders, then elaborated in the fourth.*

Plate 30. *Echoing borders change in dimensions and placement of the dark velvet triangle in Michael's Quilt.*

Plate 31. *Jean's Quilt relies on the subtle asymmetry of an odd-center medallion, balanced with striped panels of differing widths cut from patchwork strips. (Quilt by Jean Rysstad.)*

Plate 32. *The patchwork points of the star-shaped Lilacs wall hanging were made by cutting and rearranging sewn-together fabric strips.*

Plate 33. *Cutting and recombining sewn-together fabric strips created the chevron borders and central diamond of Tony's Boat Quilts. The quilting was done in spirals. (Quilts by Peggy Carl.)*

Plate 34. *An arrowhead motif emerged in Starwindow when the chevron-shaped beginnings of a star were turned around accidentally.*

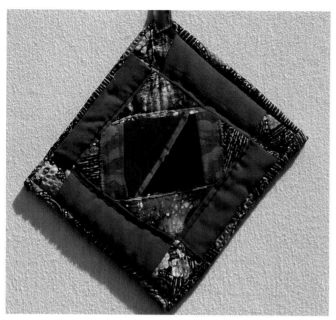

Plate 35. *In Shelia's Potholder, pink velvet narrowly bisects the center of an intricate pattern. (Potholder by Sheila Dobie.)*

Plate 37. *Assorted patchwork borders open up new possibilities for color combinations in Red Triangle.*

Plate 36. *The octagonal shape adds interest to the small medallion of Let's Imagine.*

Plate 38. *In Desire's Inferno, radiating strips stream outward from a diamond-shaped medallion constructed of two dissimilar patchwork triangles.*

Plate 39. *This detail of Desire's Inferno highlights a bit of three-dimensional sculpturing.*

Plate 40. *Somberly radiant and formally asymmetrical, an inner star of intense violet floats on an outer star of deep purple. Variations of medallion techniques were used to construct Deep Purple Star.*

Plate 41. *An example of how you might transform a square into a star is found in the design sequence for Deep Purple Star.*

Plate 42. *The Blue Medallion changed its shape several times before reaching completion.*

Plate 44. *A chain-stitched fan marks the corner of Ghislaine's Quilt, which was quilted with blue, red, gold, pink, and green thread. (Quilt by Ghislaine de St. Venant.)*

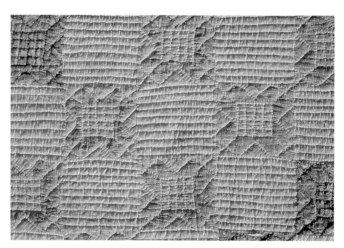

Plate 45. *Lines of quilting an inch apart have kept the cotton batting in place through a century of Antique Star's use.*

Plate 43. *A knitted lace doily serves as the focal point for Lucy's Star Quilt, as seen in this design sequence.*

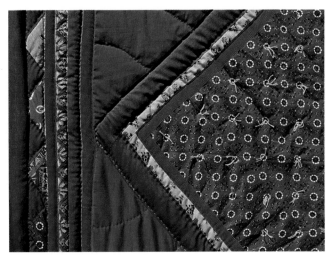

Plate 46. *Little tufts of yellow spark the flowered fabric of Nancy's Quilt and give variety to the quilting, as seen in this detail.*

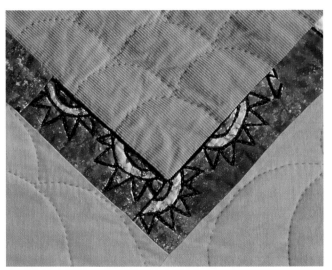

Plate 47. *Quilted starry arcs of blue are evident in this Afternoon in Paradise detail. Their shape is repeated with clamshell pattern quilting.*

Plate 48. *This detail of Afternoon in Paradise shows that each petal in this flowered medallion is outlined and defined with thread of contrasting color.*

Plate 49. *Trapunto quilting makes the butterflies spring away from the surface of the quilt in this detail of Yellow Butterfly.*

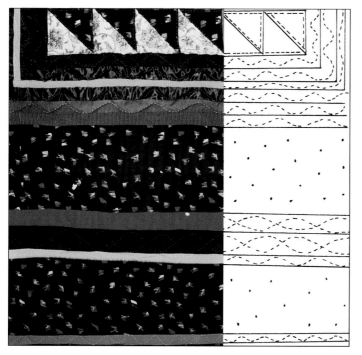

Plate 50. *As seen in this Midnight detail, knotting can be as integral to the quilting design as the lines of stitching.*

Plate 51. *Rays of quilting brighten the plain background of Ember's Quilt.*

Plate 53. *Triangles are outlined crisply with straight stitching in this detail of Midnight. The curved lines of quilting soften the border strips.*

Plate 52. *The inner medallion floats tranquilly on a wavy blue sea in Stu's Quilt.*

Plate 54. *Quilted comets flash on midnight blue satin in Mia's Quilt. Lines of quilting extend beyond the plaid into neighboring borders and multicolored zig-zag quilting echoes red-and-yellow lightning-bolt borders. (Quilt by Digby Island Quilters and friends.)*

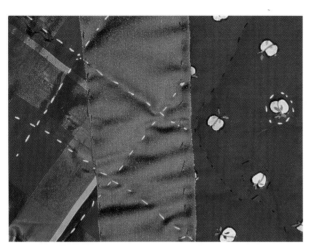

Plate 55. *In this detail of Mia's Quilt, the geometry of plaid suggested straight lines of quilting until another quilter deemed it boring and started circling apples.*

Plate 56. *A glance at the back of Mia's Quilt confirms that this is not traditional quilting, as it shows a dizzying variety of colors, designs, and stitches.*

Plate 57. *Machine quilting feathers this bird in this Bird Star detail.*

Plate 58. *Sign and date your quilts, as a way of personalizing and preserving them. Here the date is embroidered in a heart on the back of Louie's Quilt. (Quilt by Peggy Carl.)*

Decide As You Sew, Design As You Go

When you were a child, did you play with your mother's box of buttons, laying out the varied and shining discs in changing patterns on the rug? At the beach, did you collect clamshells, pine cones, and bits of colored glass, then spend the afternoon arranging and rearranging your treasures on the sand? Do you lay out patterns of pennies or paper clips on the desk, or move the objects on the kitchen windowsill until they look just so?

Decide As You Sew

These familiar activities are good training for designing a patchwork medallion quilt with decide-as-you-sew quiltmaking techniques. Designing as you go is just like playing with the box of buttons; a patchwork medallion evolves as you arrange and change and rearrange. Designing as you go, and deciding as you sew, you play with bits of fabric instead of shells and pine cones.

Throughout this book, the focus is on making design decisions border by border as you come to them, instead of planning and designing beforehand. A medallion quilt develops from the center, with each border being sewn on in turn. There is no need to plan it out on graph paper if you can let it grow and change. If you are flexible in your design expectations, there is little need for precise measuring, as borders of varying widths can be used to make everything fit.

Useful attributes for decide-as-you-sew patchwork are a tendency to arrange and rearrange, a delight in changing patterns, a patient playfulness, and the acceptance of unexpected beauty. It's not too hard; you've been doing it all your life!

Design Sequences

This chapter makes use of what I call "design sequences." Plate 23 shows sequential photographs of a quilt as it appears at different stages of its development (See Plate 23, Sweet Baby Jane, design sequence).

1. A pink-and-blue center is bordered with a dainty sprigged pastel. The next border of flowery black triangles enlivens the rather conventional beginning.

When I am working on a problem, I never think about beauty. I think only how to solve the problem. But when I have finished, if the solution is not beautiful, then I know it is wrong.

— Buckminster Fuller

2. A pale flowery frame follows, then softly vibrant handwoven plaid triangles.

3. The three outer borders are rounded and puffy, with extra batting inside.

Design sequences are included to show how a quilt progresses and grows, unfurling like a flower in the process of blooming. Because the sequences use photos of finished quilts, they show the quilting, which would not actually be there as the quilt top is being constructed.

Fabric Choice Is the First Step in Design

Hopefully you have been saving fabric: sewing scraps, old clothes, new yardages, special bits and pieces. If you haven't, chances are you know someone who has, someone who will probably be happy to let you pick through her scrap bag.

Sort through all your fabric, and pull out anything that appeals to you. Don't worry about whether the fabrics go together, and don't worry about the sizes of the pieces. Focus on picking out the fabrics that you like at this moment in time.

Make a big pile of your fabrics, and then begin acquainting yourself with your choices. Let your hands feel the different textures while your eyes move among the patterns and colors. Let your heart respond to the varied moods of the fabrics and to the sentimental remembrances that some of your scraps and old clothes may evoke. Let your mind take note that you have eight square inches of this fabric, one and one-half yards of that, and just the tiniest bit of the fabric you love the very most.

Size Determines Use

The size of a piece of fabric often determines its place in the design. Consider choosing that tiny, treasured scrap for the very center of the medallion, where the eye will focus first. Small pieces of fabric are best used in the first few borders, because as the medallion grows, the borders get bigger.

Your smallest scraps and snippets are often the most interesting and alluring fabrics and are probably the most appealing to you, if only because you have saved and cherished them so long. Using them early in the process will give the inner medallion a strong visual and emotional impact, and will set the mood and tone for later developments.

Larger yardages may of course be cut into small pieces, but perhaps they should be saved for use in the outer borders, where bigger pieces are usually needed.

Don't Use Fabric You Don't Like

Because thrift is often associated with patchwork, people sometimes feel tempted to "use up" fabric they don't like by putting it in a quilt. This is poor economy; you will end up with a quilt you don't like.

The Medallion Readily Changes Shape

In the world of medallion patchwork, a square is not always a square, because the medallion changes shape with ease (Plate 24, Quilts in Garden). Don't hesitate to let your medallion change its form.

A Square Becomes a Diamond

This is probably the most common transformation in medallion patchwork, often repeated again and again as the medallion grows. The drawing shows a square becoming diamond shaped when surrounded by four triangles, and the diamond then being changed to a square by the next border of four more triangles (See Illustration 5-1).

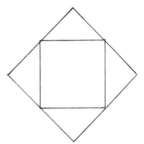

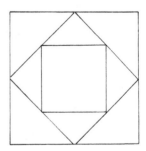

5-1. *A square becomes a diamond, and then a square again.*

A Square Becomes a Rectangle

A square can be elongated to a rectangle with strips of fabric at opposite ends. A rectangle can also be made by putting narrow borders on two sides of the square and wide borders on the other two sides (Illustration 5-2).

A Rectangle Turns Back into a Square

Adding wider borders on two sides will change a rectangle back into a square (Illustration 5-3).

A Rectangle Becomes a Diamond

Putting small triangles on the two shorter sides of a rectangle, and larger triangles on the two long sides, will create a tilted square, or diamond (Illustration 5-4).

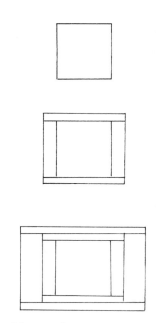

5-2. *You can change a square into a rectangle.*

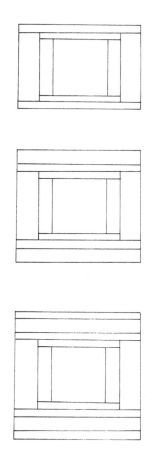

5-3. *A rectangle returns to a square when wide borders are added to two sides.*

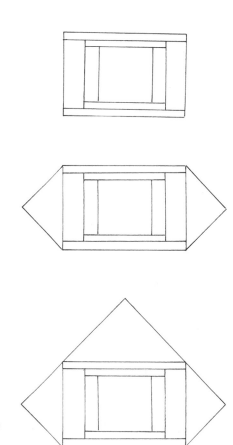

5-4. *A rectangle becomes a diamond by adding small triangles to narrow sides and large triangles to wide sides.*

A Rectangle or a Square Changes to a Hexagon

Putting triangles on two ends of a square or rectangle will produce a hexagonal lozenge, which can then be framed with strips of fabric (Illustration 5-5).

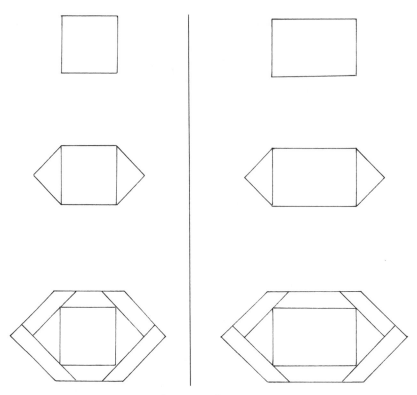

5-5. *See how a rectangle or square becomes a hexagon.*

A Hexagon Returns to a Rectangle

Filling in the four empty corners of a hexagon with small triangles will reproduce a square or rectangle (Illustration 5-6).

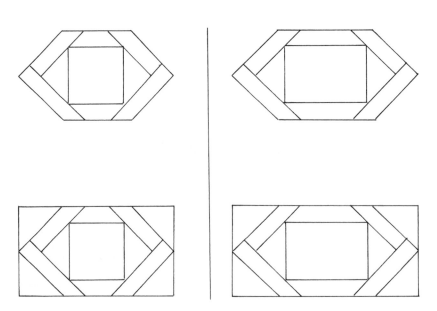

5-6. *Small triangles change the hexagon into a square or rectangle.*

A Hexagon Changes to a Diamond

Adding larger triangles to the top and bottom of a hexagonal lozenge will turn it into a diamond or tilted square (Illustration 5-7).

A Square Becomes an Octagon

Octagons can be formed by cutting the ends of fabric strips at forty-five degrees instead of ninety degrees (Illustration 5-8).

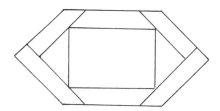

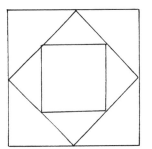

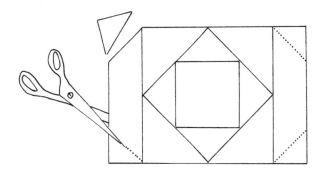

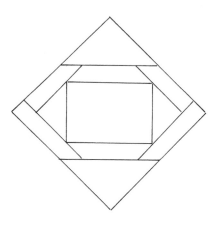

5-7. *Larger triangles turn the hexagon into a diamond.*

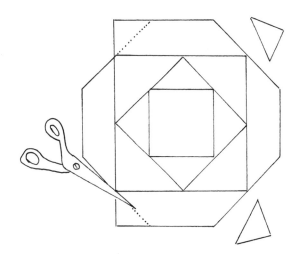

5-8. *Squares become octagons.*

Patchwork strips composed of small triangles can also be used to create octagonal medallions (Illustration 5-9).

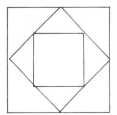
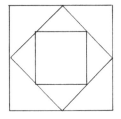
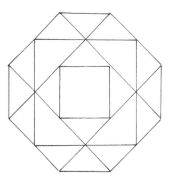
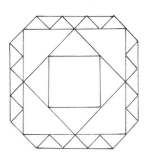

5-9. *Patchwork strips create octagons.*

An Octagon Returns to a Square

Adding a triangle to every other side of an octagon will bring it back to a square (Illustration 5-10).

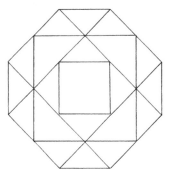
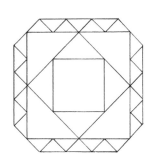
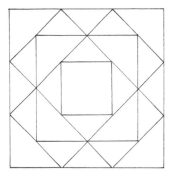
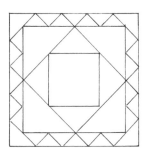

5-10. *An octagon returns to a square when triangles are added to every other side.*

Try a Different Angle

A square will always come back to a square, if it is surrounded by right triangles that have their ninety-degree angles on the outer corners. Most of your patchwork will probably be built with the familiar ninety-degree isosceles triangles shown on the left; but it is fun to experiment with triangles of a different shape, like those on the right (Illustration 5-11).

Intricate Designs Evolve from Complexly Patterned Fabric

Thoughtful placement of fabric to utilize its printed or woven patterns and motifs can produce sophisticated and complicated designs with a minimal amount of cutting and sewing. As these two quilts show, intricate designs can be developed in this way using very basic border techniques.

Mama's Sunflower

Visually complex, this small quilt was quite simply made in nine borders of very active and highly patterned fabric (Illustration 5-12).

Plate 25 details the design sequence for Mama's Sunflower (Plate 25, Mama's Sunflower, design sequence).

1. A vivid sunflower peeking over a deep red triangle is encircled by three concentric borders.
2. An energetic purple-and-red border print further activates the design.
3. The compelling yellow-and-brown print is repeated in four large corner triangles. The strips of blue-patterned fabric at top and bottom echo an earlier border.

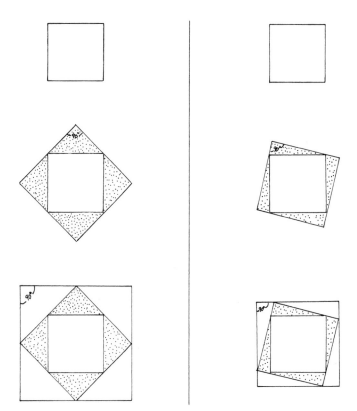

5-11. *Experiment with different angles.*

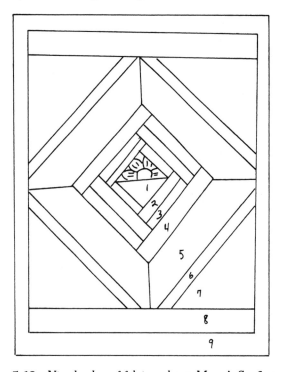

5-12. *Nine borders of fabric make up Mama's Sunflower.*

The quilting on Mama's Sunflower, shown on page 122, emphasizes the patterns of the printed fabrics by sculpting the floral motifs and outlining the triangles. Knots are tied in the center of each of the yellow motifs in the outer brown border.

Stairway

The great depth and detail in this quilt are illusions of the fabric from which it was created. The quilt was sewn in a fast and easy progression of simple strip borders, but careful deliberation was given to the dimensions of each border to utilize the fabrics for maximum visual impact.

Plate 26 highlights the design sequence for Stairway (Plate 26, Stairway, design sequence). A descending stairway is suggested by judicious choice of fabric in this simply sewn quilt. Each border is constructed by sewing strips of red fabric to two sides of the medallion, then sewing strips of dark fabric to the top and bottom of the medallion. This format is repeated again and again to build the staircase.

Echoing and Enlarging the Design

Concentric repetitions of a patchwork theme are an effective design strategy. Each time a border is echoed, it is, of course, enlarged as well.

Bird Star Quilt

The patchwork star, the speckled beige background, and the black hexagonal-square border of the inner medallion are precisely echoed in a second larger medallion that encompasses it (Plate 27, Bird Star, center; and Plate 28, Bird Star).

Scarlet and Violet Quilt

The impact of this quilt relies on the echoing of patchwork borders and the repetitive use of a limited number of fabrics in the borders that frame the patchwork motifs (Plate 29, Scarlet and Violet).

Patchwork borders are replicated with slight variations to develop a complex design, as shown in this sequence of drawings (Illustrations 5-13, 5-14, 5-15, and 5-16).

Michael's Quilt

A similar triangular patchwork element is repeated and enlarged in four concentric borders. The position of the dark velvet triangle reverses with each repetition, and each border is outlined with a vivid yellow band (Plate 30, Michael's Quilt).

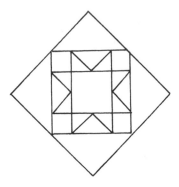

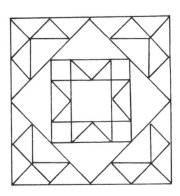

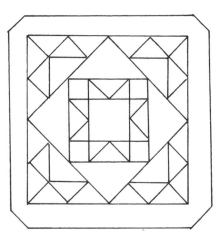

5-13. *A simple square grows into an octagonal medallion.*

5-14. *Triangles take the medallion to a diamond, and a plain border highlights the complex design.*

5-15. *A complementary border echoes the central medallion.*

5-16. *Strips create a nice contrast to the triangles that make up the rest of the medallion.*

Cut and Combine

Both Seminole quilting and rotary cutter strip-piecing techniques systematically cut and rearrange sewn-together fabric strips to form complicated patterns. The more impromptu method of decide-as-you-sew quilt-making invites cutting and recombining as well.

Jean's Quilt

Following her intuition, Jean Rysstad combined a fabric of printed stripes with sewn-together fabric strips, then cut and rearranged the pieces around a center medallion (Plate 31, Jean's Quilt).

Jean started her quilt in conventional medallion style, a hot-pink center bordered by strips of green fabric and then by black triangles (Illustration 5-17).

5-17. *This square begins Jean's Quilt.*

Rectangles side-step up the next border (Illustration 5-18).

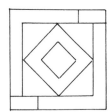

5-18. *Rectangles side-step one another in this border.*

The medallion deviates from the traditional with a random but careful arrangement of varicolored strips of fabric in several succeeding borders, held in place with a wide black border (Illustration 5-19).

Two narrow borders of varying colors follow (Illustration 5-20).

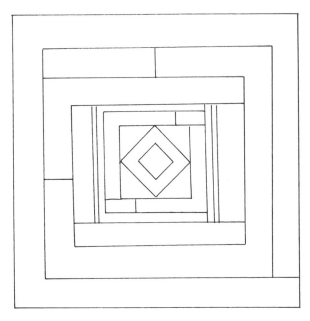

5-19. *The succeeding borders are random and irregular, but carefully placed.*

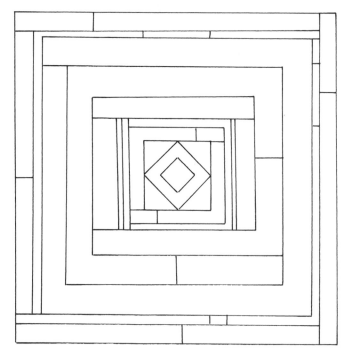

5-20. *Two narrow borders of varying colors follow.*

For the unusual outer borders, Jean sewed strips of fabric together to create a striped rectangle, then cut the rectangle into three separate striped panels (Illustration 5-21).

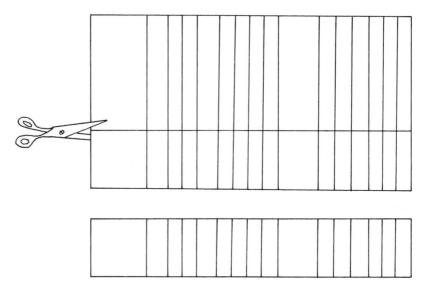

5-21. *Sewn-together fabric strips create a rectangle, which was cut into three separate panels.*

One panel of strips was sewn to the right side of the medallion, and one to the bottom. Instead of cutting the remaining piece into two narrower panels to frame the medallion symmetrically, Jean sewed this larger panel to the left side of the medallion. A final, wide, black border emphasizes the brilliant equilibrium achieved in this unusual quilt (Illustration 5-22).

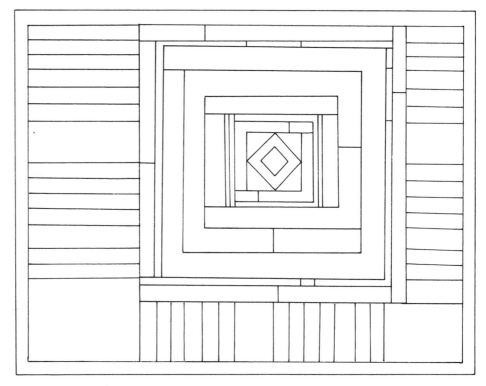

5-22. *Striped borders were sewn to three sides of the medallion, then circled with a final border.*

Lilacs Wall Hanging

This small wall hanging was created with a vaguely Seminole technique of cutting and recombining (Plate 32, Lilacs wall hanging).

Three strips of fabric were sewn together, then marked for cutting into four rectangles, then marked again to yield four long, striped isosceles triangles (Illustration 5-23).

When cut, each rectangle gave a tall isosceles triangle and two narrow mirror-imaged right triangles (Illustration 5-24).

The narrow right triangles were turned upside down and rejoined to the sides of the isosceles triangle, to form the points of a star. Very small triangles had to be added to the bases of the right triangles to complete the shape properly (Illustration 5-25).

The four patchwork points create a starry diamond around the center medallion (Illustration 5-26).

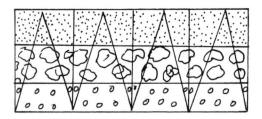

5-23. *Four triangles emerge from three strips of fabric that had been sewn together.*

5-24. *Each rectangle provides a tall isosceles triangle and two right triangles.*

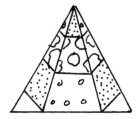

5-25. *Right triangles (with small additions at bases) are turned upside down and sewn to isosceles triangle.*

5-26. *Four patchwork points form a starry diamond around the center medallion.*

Tony's Boat Quilts

The quilt shown below is part of a set of bedding made by Peggy Carl to fit a boat berth (Plate 33, Tony's Boat quilts). Cutting and recombining, she created patchwork designs for a quilt, a sleeping bag cover, a mattress pad, and pillowcases.

Peggy, who says she has a "definite preference for not planning ahead," tore her fabric into strips and sewed the strips together to form an expanse of fabric from which diagonal strips were then marked and cut (Illustration 5-27).

Two mirror-image sets of diagonal strips were cut, leaving large striped triangles, which were also mirror images of each other (Illustration 5-28).

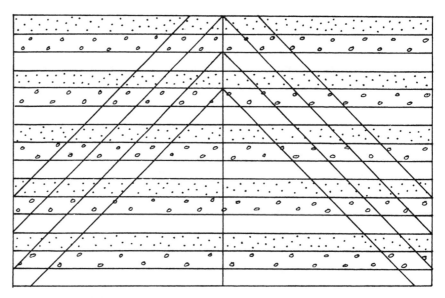

5-27. *The quiltmaker tore fabric into strips, sewed them together, and then cut diagonal strips.*

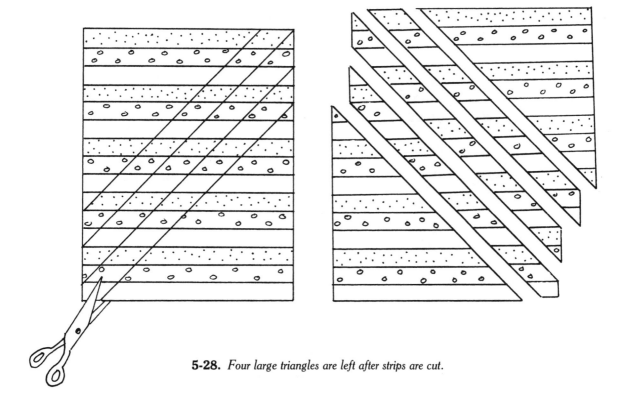

5-28. *Four large triangles are left after strips are cut.*

The chevron zig-zag borders at top and bottom were formed by sandwiching a diagonal strip cut from one side of the fabric between two diagonal strips cut from the other side.

Two of the large striped triangles were turned and combined to form the diamond in the center of the quilt (Illustration 5-29). The remaining triangles were used in decorating the other pieces of bedding.

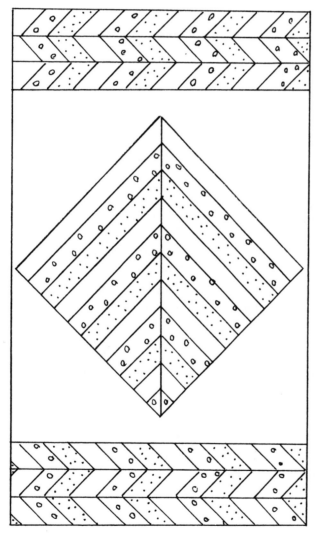

5-29. *A diamond results from joining two of the large striped triangles.*

Turn it Around or Upside Down

It is always interesting to change the orientation of a patchwork unit before it is sewn down, just in case it is more effective in its new position than in the one for which you had planned.

Starwindow

I discovered the intriguing adaptability of patchwork units by accident when I casually reversed four patchwork pieces and saw a new pattern emerge. I had constructed four arrowheads, which I intended to use in forming a star (Illustration 5-30). When I nonchalantly turned the arrowheads end on end, a dramatic new shape startled me (Illustration 5-31).

A further inspiration suggested that four patchwork squares I had constructed for a different project would fit in the four corners of the cross (Illustration 5-32).

I was surprised by the unexpected and exciting patchwork medallion I had so cleverly and accidentally created by turning my patchwork pieces around (Plate 34, Starwindow).

As I constructed the medallion, I saw yet another possible variation from the same patchwork pieces. By dividing the elements of the medallion differently, a flower basket motif emerged (Illustration 5-33).

5-30. *These four arrowheads were intended for a star.*

5-31. *But turning the arrowheads end on end creates a new shape.*

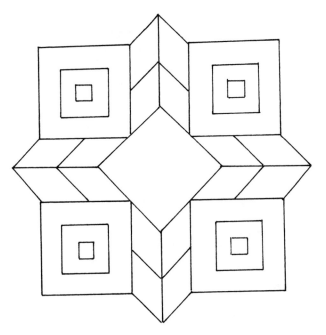

5-32. *Four patchwork squares intended for another project fit in the four corners of the cross.*

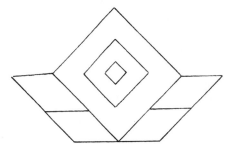

5-33. *A flower basket emerges from the medallion.*

Stop When It's Done

Not every medallion has to become a king-size quilt. If you have created a small masterpiece, don't struggle trying to make it bigger.

Shiela's Potholder

Tiny scraps of treasured fabric were combined by Shiela Dobie into a spectacularly ceremonial velvet and batik potholder (Plate 35, Shiela's Potholder).

Let's Imagine Wall Hanging

Remember being asked to imagine a number of design possibilities for different arrangements of triangles around a medallion in the "Introduction"? Here is how the medallion ended up (Plate 36, Let's Imagine wall hanging).

Change the Rules

Rules are made to be broken, and it makes life more interesting and the design more dynamic if you feel free to change the rules during the construction of a repetitively patterned quilt.

Red Triangle Quilt

I began the quilt by forming a central medallion of twenty patchwork squares and then surrounded it by three concentric patchwork borders. For each border, I changed the rules on how the colors of the patchwork squares were arranged (Plate 37, Red Triangle, design sequence).

Here are the steps involved:

1. Twenty similar patchwork squares with red triangles at the bottom were sewn together.
2. Changing the rules, the patchwork squares for the next border had either purple triangles or red triangles facing each other.
3. The rules changed again to compose the two outer borders with patchwork squares, each having one purple triangle. The orientation of the squares was changed in the last border so all the purple triangles point outward.

When I began making the small patchwork squares for the Red Triangle quilt, my rules were to have two similar triangles facing each other, with a red triangle at the bottom and a contrasting triangle at the top (Illustration 5-34).

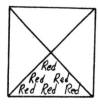

5-34. *Red Triangle started with a center of twenty patchwork squares, each with a red triangle at the bottom (see picture 1 of design sequence, Plate 37).*

But I was bored with this by the time I had constructed twenty squares and sewn them into a rectangle, so I changed the rules. My next border was composed of small patchwork squares in two variations, either top and bottom triangles of red with contrasting side triangles, or top and bottom triangles of purple with contrasting side triangles (Illustration 5-35).

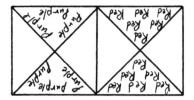

5-35. *Surrounding the twenty-square center is a border that alternates "hour glass" pairs of triangles in red or purple (see picture 2 of design sequence, Plate 37).*

My rule for the next border was to make the small patchwork squares with a purple triangle at the bottom, two similar triangles at the sides, and a contrasting triangle at the top (Illustration 5-36).

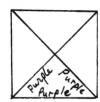

5-36. *Each of the patchwork squares of the next concentric border has a purple triangle at the bottom.*

For the last border, I wanted a frame of purple triangles pointing outward all around the quilt, so my small patchwork triangles were sewn with purple on one side and a red floral opposite, and two similar triangles facing each other on the other sides. I placed the squares so the points of all the purple triangles faced outward (Illustration 5-37).

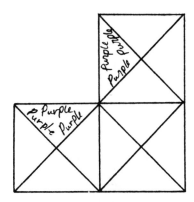

5-37. *The points of all the purple triangles face outward in the last border (see picture 3 of design sequence, Plate 37).*

Go to Extremes

A medallion will sometimes develop a life of its own and drag you kicking and screaming in a direction you had not anticipated. You might as well relax and enjoy the ride, because an extraordinary design is probably in the process of creation.

Desire's Inferno Quilt

This quilt began quite staidly with a red triangle, which I enlarged with a border of fabric strips sewn log-cabin style to its three sides. One border led to another and another until the red triangle was three deep in borders (Illustration 5-38).

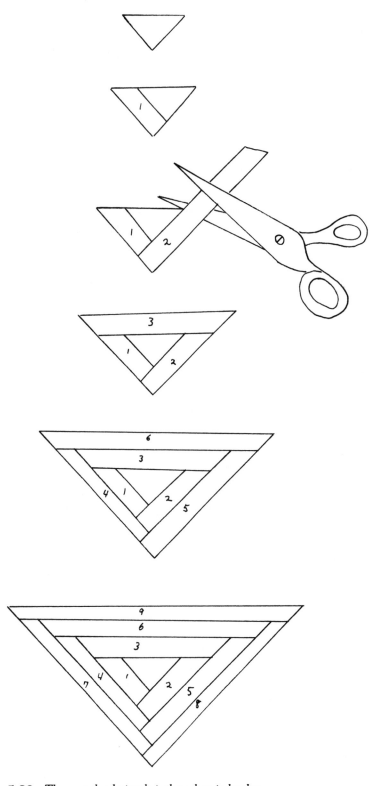

5-38. *The central red triangle is three deep in borders.*

83

The other half of the central medallion started with a square made from two small triangles. On two sides of this square, log cabin half-borders were added, forming a larger square. Triangles made from fabric strips were sewn to the other two sides of the square, creating a larger triangle of elaborate patchwork (Illustration 5-39).

The two triangles were then joined together (Illustration 5-40).

5-40. *Two triangles are joined together.*

5-39. *An asymmetrically constructed square is flanked by triangles.*

Four sets of concentric borders were added to encircle and complete the central medallion. As the numbers indicating their order of placement show, they were sewn on concentrically, in a kind of square "spiral" (Illustration 5-41).

5-41. *Four sets of concentric borders are sewn on in a "square spiral."*

Now envisioning an outer border of radiating strips, I laid the inner medallion on the floor and drew a large rectangle around it and then made a newspaper pattern for each of the four corners that would need to be filled in. As I sewed the strips together, I laid the patchwork on top of the newspaper pattern to make sure it was shaping up correctly.

Using sewing scraps and recycled clothing, I had lots of tapering strips, which were used with the wide end outward. The strips went beyond the edge of the pattern in a raggedy fringe, which was later trimmed off evenly (Illustration 5-42).

It took a bit of fussing to get the radiating strips sewn in place around the central medallion, but when that was done, the quilt top was finished with four concentric borders of solid-colored fabric (Plate 38, Desire's Inferno).

The dense sculptural quilting in the center medallion came about by accident, as the solution to a very big problem. I had quilted without a frame and never thought to spread the quilt out flat during the process. When I laid the finished quilt out on the bed to admire it, I realized with a sinking heart that the outer radiating strips had been quilted much tighter than the central medallion. This left the center terribly loose and floppy, and distressingly makeshift in appearance.

After several days I came up with a solution. The quilt was turned over, a pyramid of batting was layered in the center, and the new batting was basted loosely to the back of the quilt. I covered this new center batting with new backing fabric, sewing it onto the old backing with tiny hand stitches. After turning the quilt to the front again, I

5-42. *Strips are trimmed evenly.*

spent several days quilting a second set of stitches in the central medallion to hold new and old layers of batting together.

This secondary quilting, done under duress, added new elements to the design of the quilt, both in a more elaborate etching of stitches and in a bolder, three-dimensional sculpturing of the surface (Plate 39, Desire's Inferno, detail).

Take to the Stars

Sewing a triangle to each side of an octagon will create an eight-pointed star. Filling in the spaces between the points will recreate the octagon.

Deep Purple Star Quilt

Symmetrical, yet faintly askew, this eight-pointed star was built from the center using variations of medallion techniques (Plate 40, Deep Purple Star). Plate 41 (Deep Purple Star design sequence) shows the design sequence, which illustrates the following steps:

1. A batik rectangle and a medley of tiny patchwork scraps are framed by uneven strips of velvet.

2. A border of brown, maroon, purple, navy blue, and flowered triangles is circled with an octagon of varied purple strips.

3. The center medallion is boldly emphasized with an eight-sided, flower-speckled, black velvet border, and then becomes a star with vividly violet points.

4. The inner star is octagonally bordered with navy blue velour, then starred again with a deep purple star.

The very center of the quilt is square, but the randomly tapered velvet strips that follow shift it off-kilter (Illustration 5-43). A border of triangles, with trapezoidal strips at the corners, changes it from a four-sided medallion to an eight-sided one (Illustration 5-44).

Strips of fabric in varying shades of purple were used to encircle the octagon. It is easier to sew a strip on first, then trim the ends to the proper angle (Illustration 5-45). Because the medallion was lopsided almost from

the very start, by the time it reached the octagonal, flower-speckled black border, each of its eight sides was of slightly different length (Illustration 5-46).

5-43. *Randomly tapered strips shift the quilt's center.*

5-44. *A four-sided medallion becomes eight-sided.*

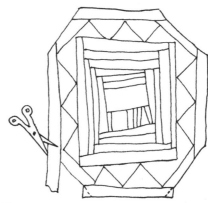

5-45. *Trim strips after sewing on.*

87

I folded and fussed with a newspaper pattern to cut eight slightly different purple star points for the inner star, then sewed them to the eight sides of the black octagonal border. Now the spaces between the star points needed filling in, so I folded newspaper again and cut eight flattened, brown-velvet fill-in triangles, which I sewed on by hand to bridge the spaces between star points. The medallion is now a larger octagon emblazoned with a purple star (Illustration 5-47).

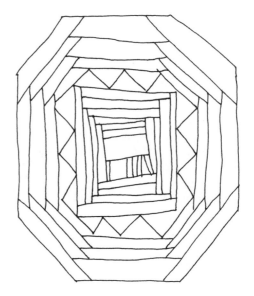

5-46. *All eight sides have different lengths.*

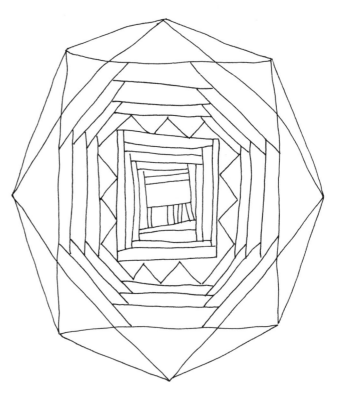

5-47. *Now the medallion is a larger octagon.*

A broad border of navy blue velour surrounds the octagon. Deep purple triangles create the points of the outer star (Illustration 5-48).

5-48. *Purple triangles form the points of the outer star.*

As I went on to make other star quilts, I learned that a more tidily geometric octagon made the sewing easier. Sewing construction is streamlined if you start with an octagonal medallion that is the same on all eight sides, and if you use right-angle isosceles triangles for the points of the star.

Four triangular star points are sewn to four alternating sides of the octagon (Illustration 5-49).

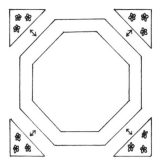

5-49. *Four triangular star points are sewn to alternating sides of the octagon.*

Attaching the four star points makes the medallion into a square temporarily. Each of the four remaining triangular star points will have a flattened fill-in triangle sewn on either side.

These units are fastened to each side of the square (Illustration 5-50). An eight-pointed star within a larger octagon has been formed.

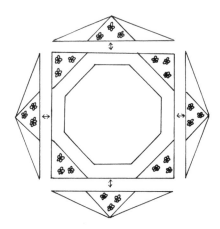

5-50. *Triangular units are attached to each side of the square.*

The first step in creating a narrow border around the octagon is to sew strips to every other side of the medallion. The illustration shows four strips of fabric attached, with the final strip being trimmed to the proper angle (Illustration 5-51).

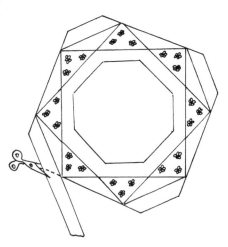

5-51. *Strips are added to every other side, then trimmed.*

Four more fabric strips are then attached to the other four sides of the octagon, and their ends are trimmed (Illustration 5-52).

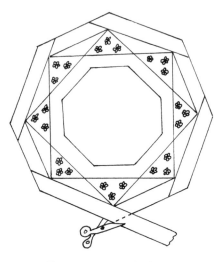

5-52. *Four more strips of fabric are attached, and their ends are trimmed.*

The process is repeated to form the outer star. First, four triangular star points are attached to every other side of the octagon, bringing the medallion back to a square (Illustration 5-53).

5-53. *The medallion is once again a square.*

Flattened fill-in triangles (Illustration 5-54) are attached to each side of the remaining triangular star points. When these units are sewn onto the medallion, a larger star appears (Illustration 5-55).

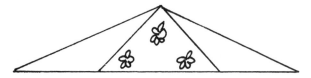

5-54. *Create four flattened fill-in triangles.*

5-55. *Adding fill-in triangles creates a larger star.*

Transformative Shifts

As I ventured beyond the square, I began experimenting with a variety of medallion forms and finally figured out how to use background or fill-in triangles of differing shapes to shift from one medallion configuration to another.

Blue Medallion

From four-sided to six-sided, to eight-sided, to twelve-pointed, to an oval, this medallion transforms from shape to shape (Plate 42, Blue Medallion).

The center of the quilt is a patchwork rectangle, turned into a long hexagon by adding triangles on either end (Illustration 5-56). The medallion is enlarged by a double border (Illustration 5-57). The hexagon is changed to a rectangle by adding patchwork triangles at the ends (Illustration 5-58). Top and bottom panels of patchwork are added, with long fill-in triangles bridging the gaps to create an eight-sided medallion (Illustration 5-59). Three concentric borders follow (Illustration 5-60). Twelve triangular patchwork points are attached, with triangular fill-ins between. The shape of the fill-ins can be figured out geometrically or by trial and error (Illustration 5-61).

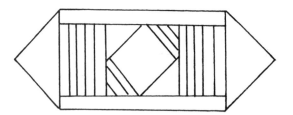

5-56. *Adding triangles to the patchwork rectangle turns it into a long hexagon.*

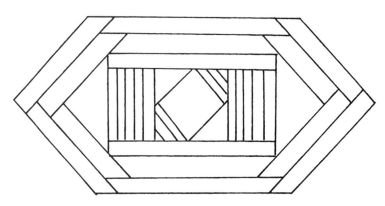

5-57. *A double border makes the medallion larger.*

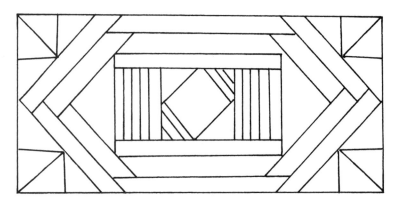

5-58. *Adding patchwork triangles to the ends of the hexagon turns it into a rectangle.*

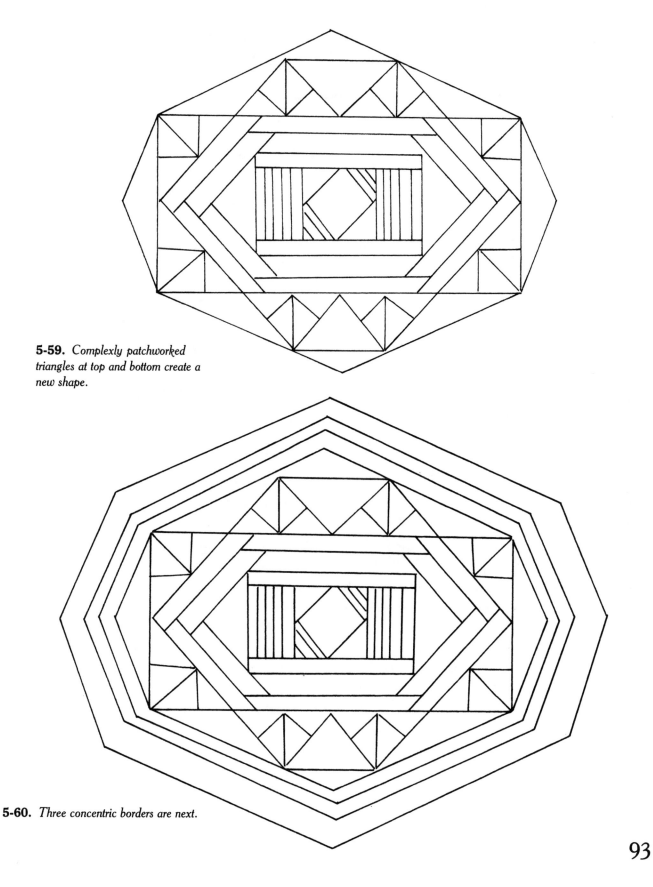

5-59. *Complexly patchworked triangles at top and bottom create a new shape.*

5-60. *Three concentric borders are next.*

5-61. *Shape of the fill-ins can be figured out geometrically, or by trial and error.*

Hexagon and Star

A six-sided design shifting between hexagon and star can be worked out with a little geometry.

Lucy's Star Quilt

Lucy had sent me the fabric for this quilt, rich, deep, solid colors and coordinated border prints. With the fabric, Lucy also sent an intricately knitted antique white lace doily, which I appliquéd onto a hexagonal piece of black velvet to become the center of a six-pointed star. Like all my quilts, this one started in the center, and one border after another was decided on and then sewn down, without preplanning or graphing. Plate 43 illustrates the following design sequence (Plate 43, Lucy's Star, design sequence):

1. Triangles surround an antique doily to shape a six-pointed star.
2. Several borders enlarge the hexagon.
3. A starburst of small triangles circles the medallion, which is then framed with strips of fabric.
4. A dazzling star is created with triangles sewn from varied strips of fabric.
5. A plain red background and wide outer borders finish the quilt.

Although the mathematics did not come easy to me, I found that this was one quilt where I needed to be as meticulous as possible in calculating the shapes I needed for each border. Rather than tortuously attempting to explain my methods, I'll suggest you review a basic geometry book, or read Katie Pasquini's *Mandala*.

But I do have a few tips for six-sided sewing. The secret is to work on three sides at a time.

Start with a hexagon (Illustration 5-62).

5-62. *Six-sided sewing begins with a hexagon.*

To attach the equilateral triangles used as the points of the star, begin by sewing three triangles to every other side of the hexagon. The medallion is now briefly triangular (Illustration 5-63).

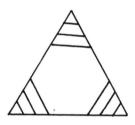

5-63. *Triangles are sewn to every other side of the hexagon, making the medallion triangular.*

Three patchwork units, each consisting of an equilateral star point with flattened triangles on either side, are now constructed.

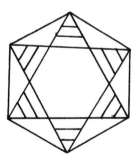

5-64. *Sew patchwork units to each of the three sides of the triangular medallion to regain the hexagon.*

These patchwork units are then sewn to each of the sides of the triangular medallion, thus regaining a hexagonal shape (Illustration 5-64).

Sewn-together strips of fabric create six flattened triangles, which are sewn to the six sides of the hexagon (Illustration 5-65).

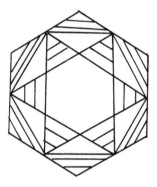

5-65. *Six flattened triangles are sewn to the six sides of the hexagon.*

Six strips of fabric form the next border (Illustration 5-66).

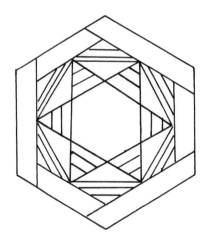

5-66. *Six strips of fabric form the next border.*

95

The hexagonal sawtooth border is constructed next. First, six patchwork units are built from small equilateral triangles. Three of these patchwork units are sewn to three sides of the hexagonal medallion (Illustration 5-67).

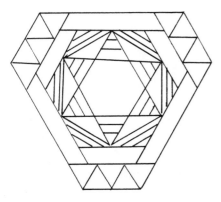

5-67. *Three patchwork units are sewn to three sides of the hexagonal medallion.*

Flattened triangles are attached to either end of each of the three remaining patchwork units. Attaching these patchwork units to the other sides of the medallion creates a twelve-sided shape (Illustration 5-68).

5-68. *Attaching three flattened triangles to the medallion creates a twelve-sided shape.*

The twelve-sided shape shifts back to a hexagon by adding six more flattened triangles (Illustration 5-69).

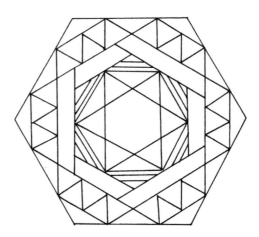

5-69. *Adding six more flattened triangles takes the shape back to a hexagon.*

The growing hexagon is again encircled by a border of strips (Illustration 5-70).

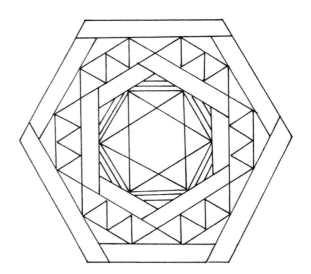

5-70. *Now the hexagon is surrounded by a border of fabric strips.*

The large outer star was constructed in the same way as the small inner one. First, six equilateral triangles were patchworked together out of strips of fabric. Three of these triangles were attached to alternate sides of the hexagon, temporarily changing the shape of the medallion to a very large triangle (Illustration 5-71).

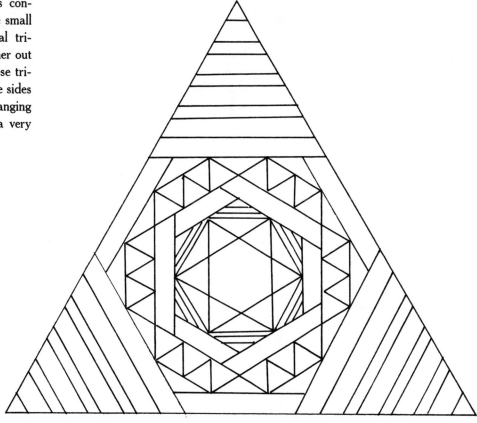

5-71. *Three equilateral patchwork triangles are attached to alternate sides of the hexagon, making the medallion a big triangle.*

Flattened triangles were sewn to either side of each of the three remaining patchwork triangles (Illustration 5-72).

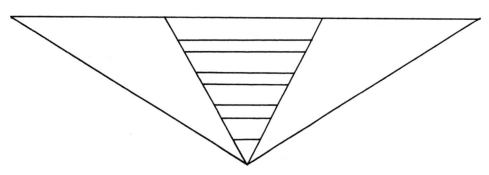

5-72. *Sew flattened triangles to either side of each of the three remaining patchwork triangles.*

97

The hexagon is again recreated with the attachment of these patchwork units, and a large star emerges (Illustration 5-73).

Never before or since have I done so much measuring and calculating, and although I was very pleased with how the quilt turned out, I vowed "never again," and gladly returned to my more haphazard and less meticulous methods. But I had two more problems to surmount before Lucy's Star was finished.

As described in the "Troubleshooting" chapter, I carelessly didn't check the underside of the quilt until I had finished quilting. Then I found a huge unquilted flap of batting and backing hanging underneath the quilt. When that problem was finally solved, the quilt seemed perfect, except. . . .

The beautiful white doily in the center seemed too stark and white, not fitting with the more muted tones of the quilt. Luckily, Lucy knew a solution. We unstitched the doily, soaked it in strong tea, dried it, and stitched it back in place. The doily's newly antiqued ecru tone now complemented the quilt perfectly.

But I needed more than a strong cup of tea to recover from my unaccustomed attempt at perfection.

5-73. *A large star emerges.*

Design Ammunition

Stockpile Triangles in Multiples Of Four

One of the simplest design strategies is to have a number of small triangles on hand for arranging around the medallion in different patterns. Most medallions are four-sided, so cut out triangles in multiples of four. Choose several of your fabrics and cut sets of four, eight, or sixteen triangles from each.

Use these triangles to develop experimental patterns by laying them out in as many different ways as you can devise. If an outstanding pattern develops, sew the triangles together and incorporate your discovery into the medallion. The triangles won't go to waste if they are not used; they can be used again and again to lay out experimental patterns and will eventually become part of a medallion.

Stockpile Patchwork Units in Multiples of Four

Also useful is a stockpile of already-sewn patchwork units. Having four, eight, or sixteen similar patchwork triangles, strips, or squares on hand allows you to experiment very quickly with a number of complex designs.

This photo shows some of the patchwork units that were left over from Nancy's Quilt (Photo 5-74).

Here are some of the ways these patchwork units could be used in later projects. The first drawing shows the small patchwork squares set in the four corners of a plain border (Illustration 5-75).

5-74. *Patchwork units left over from Nancy's Quilt.*

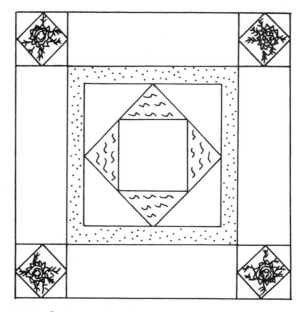

5-75. *Leftover patchwork squares might have been used in the four corners of a plain border.*

99

The next drawing shows the same central medallion, now framed by the three-triangle patchwork units, which change its shape to an octagon (Illustration 5-76).

5-76. *Framing the central medallion with three-triangle patchwork units turns it into an octagon.*

In the third drawing, the central medallion is surrounded by the large triangles with fabric strips at their base (Illustration 5-77).

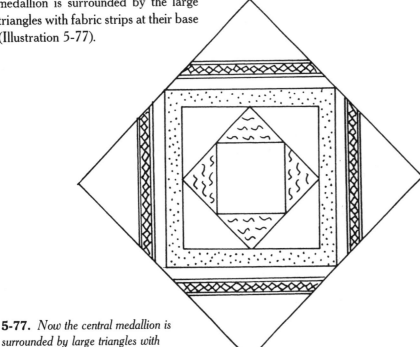

5-77. *Now the central medallion is surrounded by large triangles with fabric strips at their base.*

Use the Same Patchwork Unit In Different Quilts

The exact same patchwork pieces can have strikingly different effects depending on how they are used. You can see this by looking at Michael's Quilt (See Plate 30) and at the Blue Medallion (See Plate 42).

I had made a dozen identical patchwork units (Illustration 5-78).

5-78. *One dozen identical patchwork units were made.*

Four of these patchwork units were used to frame the central medallion of Michael's Quilt (Illustration 5-79).

5-79. *Four patchwork units frame the central medallion of Michael's Quilt.*

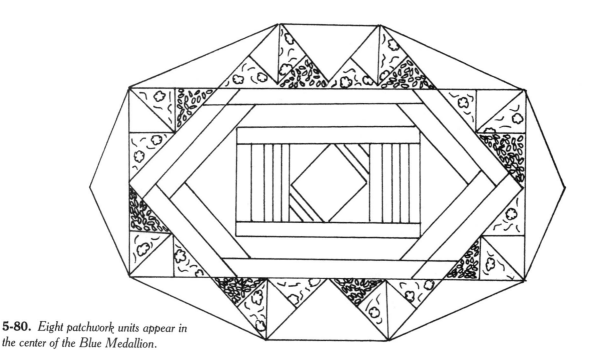

5-80. *Eight patchwork units appear in the center of the Blue Medallion.*

The eight remaining patchwork units were used, with a quite different effect, in the central medallion of the Blue Medallion quilt (Illustration 5-80).

Whenever you make a number of patchwork units, take a few minutes to play with them experimentally, devising as many varying patterns as you can.

Don't consider it wasted effort if you make a number of patchwork units for a project but then decide not to use them. They will soon be utilized in a different project.

Work on Multiple Medallions

I often have several dozen medallions on the go at once, in various stages of completion. When I'm stymied by one project, I'll work on another. Some never get finished; some turn into masterpieces. Quite often, the patchwork elements I thought I made for one medallion become incorporated into another medallion.

Choose from the Mistake Basket

Don't forget the exciting possibilities lurking in the basket or drawer where you throw your mistakes and rejects. If you save all patchwork pieces that were sewn together but not used, you will have a handy supply of ready-made patchwork choices. When you feel uncertain about the next border, try a few candidates from your "mistake basket." Even if there is nothing suitable, considering these patchwork complexities will give you fresh ideas and inspiration.

Tricks of the Trade

Look for the Zap

You may have felt the "zap" when a particular bolt of fabric leapt to your gaze across a crowded fabric store. That sudden "Aha!" when you hold two fabrics together and they look absolutely great is the zap.

The zap is an intuitive message, a visual click, a bonk on the head that says you've got it right. Trust your zaps! Seek them out by trying different possibilities and noticing your own reactions.

I don't have a word for the opposite of the zap, but it too is a real feeling and should not be ignored. If a design or fabric choice gives you a dreary ho-hum, find something else.

Back Away

As the medallion gets bigger, it becomes more important to distance yourself from it periodically. Moving away from your design lets you see it in its entirety and makes it easier to decide what comes next.

Lay the medallion on the floor and climb on a chair to see it from a greater distance and a new perspective.

Hang your patchwork on the wall and leave the room; come back in and surprise yourself with a new viewpoint on your work.

Turn your back on your quilt, then catch an unexpected glimpse of it by looking over your shoulder with a mirror. Focusing on your quilt through the wrong end of binoculars or a telescope may seem silly, but it will give you the distance needed to view it objectively.

Try out Fabric Possibilities

Spread out a piece of fabric that you are considering for the next border, and lay the medallion on top of it to see how it looks. Do this with several different fabrics until you find one that clicks. Then decide how best to use that fabric. Or pin the medallion on the wall, and pin strips or triangles of fabric around it.

Take Time to Decide

You might leave an unfinished quilt on the wall for weeks before suddenly seeing a wonderful possibility for the next border. After months of glaring at an unsatisfactory medallion, you may finally find the perfect solution to the problem. Patchwork keeps, and

there is no harm in putting a frustrating project away for a while.

Invite Comment

If you've been agonizing endlessly over a fabric choice or a design decision, maybe it's time to ask someone else's opinion. This person doesn't have to be a quiltmaker or a designer; any friend, neighbor, or discerning child will do. If you make it clear that you are seeking suggestions rather than compliments, you will probably be given a new perspective on the problem. The answer may be unexpected. You don't have to take the offered advice, but inviting comment gives opportunity to see your work with a fresh and unbiased eye.

Design with a Capital D?

This chapter has been a hard one to write, because I don't normally think or talk much about design. I just make quilts. I can't say "Do it this way," when the message I want to convey most strongly is "Do it your own way." Intuition, imagination, and the willingness to take a risk are more important than principles or rules of design. My best advice: Don't take design too seriously.

Don't Quit Till It's Quilted

Making the patchwork top is the exciting and glamorous part of quilt-making. Doing the quilting can be boring and tedious, calling on all our reserves of patience and diligence. Why do we bother?

Endless Stitches

What is Quilting For?

Quilting is very important, as it gives strength and durability by reinforcing the seams of the patchwork top and thus prevents strain on them. A quilt that is closely quilted with strong thread will last many years longer than one that is not, so it is worth the time and effort. The quilting stitches prevent things from shifting about by fastening together the patchwork top, the batting, and the backing fabric.

Aesthetically, the lines of quilting enhance the beauty of the patchwork design. Quilting takes your design from a flat, two-dimensional pattern to a sculptured, three-dimensional surface with depth, texture, and shadow.

Size of Stitch

Trying to match the twelve stitches to the inch recommended by traditional quilters can be frustrating. I would advise you not to try. Use strong thread, do your best, and don't judge your results too harshly.

You are bound to be discouraged if you compare your first attempts at quilting with the beautifully precise work you might see on an antique quilt. Two hundred years ago, women had a mastery of hand sewing that we do not usually match today. From early childhood, females were trained in sewing by hand, with the household largely dependent on their skills with needle and thread to provide the family's bedding and clothing. Your skills and training as a modern woman are very different, and it is unlikely that you will ever recreate the tiny and meticulous stitches of the past.

Because your stitches are likely to be large, why not use them to emphasize the design, choosing beautifully colored crochet thread, perl cotton, buttonhole twist, or embroidery floss instead of the more traditional thin, white cotton quilting thread? Choose strong threads with a lively presence, and use them to etch an added layer of beauty onto your quilt.

The stitching on Ghislaine's Quilt

It is as scandalous for a woman not to know how to use her needle as it is for a man not to know how to use his sword.

—Lady Mary Wortley Montague

(See Plate 44, Ghislaine's Quilt, quilting detail) is vibrant, energetic, and amusing. The robust threads she chose interact brightly with the patchwork design.

Don't Skimp on Quilting

Although I'm telling you not to be too fussy about the size of your stitches, I am not suggesting that you skimp on the amount of quilting you do. We are lucky to have the polyester quilt batt, which requires far less quilting than the old-fashioned cotton batt; but even so, it may feel as though an endless number of stitches are required before your quilt is finished.

As a general rule, don't leave any area larger than the palm of your hand unquilted. The quilting stitch builds in strength, durability, beauty, and longevity. Patience pays in quilting: you will reap what you sew.

Tools and Supplies for Quilting

The Finished Quilt Top

Inspect the seams and make any needed repairs. Iron the top well, or put it in the dryer with a damp towel to remove wrinkles.

The Backing

It is easiest to use a bed sheet for the back, though several lengths of narrow fabric can be sewn together instead. Choose a soft yet strong fabric, preferably cotton, as blends or synthetics may be harder to stitch through, and you have lots of stitches to sew.

Choose a color that suits the patchwork top, especially if the backing is to be folded to the front to bind the quilt. Patterned fabric may be used as a backing, but a solid fabric will

better display the sculptured beauty of your quilting stitches.

Decide the method of binding the edges now (see pages 132–134), and calculate the dimensions of the backing. If in doubt, give yourself a little extra fabric. If you have prewashed all the fabrics used in the quilt top, then prewash the backing as well. Get rid of wrinkles by ironing or by fluffing in the dryer with a damp towel.

Batting/Batt

The thinner the batting, the easier it is to take small, even stitches. A thicker batting will be harder to stitch, but will provide a warm and puffy quilt.

Polyester batting: For general all-around convenience, the polyester or dacron batt has several advantages. It washes easily without coming apart, dries quickly, and needs much less quilting than the traditional cotton quilt batt. A medium-weight bonded polyester batt is easy to work with. Bonding is a manufacturing process that coats the surface of the batt with a glaze. This makes the batt easier to handle, as it will stay in one piece instead of shredding apart while it is being laid out. The glaze also prevents bits of batting from working their way to the surface of the quilt through the needle holes.

Cotton batting: An all-cotton quilt has a lovely feel and a special smooth suppleness that is not found in other quilts. It's easy to quilt because cotton accepts the needle nicely. But the cotton quilt batt requires extremely close and generous quilting. If quilted too sparsely, the batting will ball up when washed, leaving hard lumps throughout the quilt. Again, a glazed surface may make handling easier.

The very extensive quilting on an antique quilt shows the extremely close stitching necessary with a cotton quilt (Plate 45, Antique Star).

Wool batting: Wool batting is luxuriantly thick and warm. Although the needle slides smoothly and easily through wool, its thickness may make it hard to take small stitches. A quilt with a wool batt should perhaps be dry-cleaned, as the batting may shrink when washed. However, advertisements for modern wool batting seem to promise easier care and washability, and some of the suppliers offer quilting tips and instructions on cleaning.

Wool batting tends to work its way to the surface of a quilt, through needle holes or even through coarse woven fabric. This can be prevented if you are able to choose a wool batt with a glazed finish, or if you encase the batting in cheesecloth.

There has been a resurgence of wool batting in recent years, and you may find a woolen batt warm and practical.

Blankets: An old wool or acrylic blanket can be used instead of batting. I recently saw an antique quilt that apparently used an even older quilt as the middle layer, for glimpses of hidden patchwork could be seen beneath torn areas of the quilt top. My mother's church quilting group, which makes quilts to be given to the homeless, takes the wires out of old electric blankets and uses the blankets in place of batting in their quilts.

Piecing a batting: If the quilt batting is smaller than what is needed, another piece can be added on. Butt the edges of the batting close to each other. Using strong thread, whipstitch the two pieces of batting together using big loose stitches and making knots

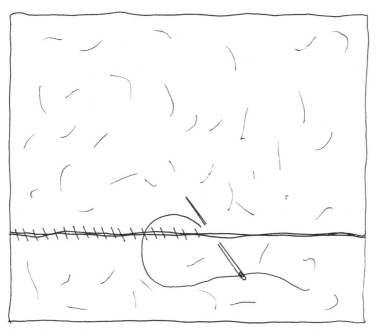

6-1. *Don't pull the thread too tight or the batting will bunch up.*

at intervals. Don't pull the thread too tight or the batting will bunch up into a ridge where it is joined (See Illustration 6-1).

Needles

Like any precision tool, the needle comes in various sizes and shapes, and you will find the task of quilting made easier by selecting a needle that suits the job. The larger the number, the smaller the needle. A thinner needle pierces the fabric more easily, but it will be harder to thread, and may break. Choose as small a needle as you are able to thread easily, because large needles are harder to force through the layers of the quilt and may leave needle holes where the batting can work through.

The between or quilting needle: This short, sturdy needle with a small eye is the traditional choice of most quilters.

The embroidery needle: I prefer a small embroidery needle (size 7, 8, or 9) for quilting, as it is slim and flexible, with a large eye.

Thread

Use a strong, good quality thread for hand quilting. Use short lengths to avoid knots and tangles. The thread is not doubled when quilting, because quilters believe that the doubled threads will rub against each other and wear out more quickly.

Cotton quilting thread: Traditionally available only in white, this strong cotton thread now comes in a rainbow of colors. It is pleasant and easy to sew with, especially if pre-waxed.

Heavy duty cotton thread: Ordinary, strong sewing thread can also be used for quilting. Wax it to avoid tangles.

Perl cotton: Once used for tatting,

this thick, smooth thread is wonderful for quilting, although quite expensive. Size 8 perl cotton from DMC comes in small, brilliantly colored balls and is hard to resist.

Tatting thread: Finer than crochet thread, and more tightly twisted than perl cotton, this somewhat antiquated thread quilts nicely and can sometimes be found in bright colors.

Crochet thread: Size 30 or finer crochet cotton is excellent for quilting and is a very strong thread.

Embroidery floss: Being a soft thread, several strands should be used for strength. Ease of sewing and a huge array of shades make embroidery thread a favorite choice. You may, of course, want to embroider on the quilt top, instead of simply quilting.

Silk buttonhole thread: If you can find this scarce and costly thread, you will have great pleasure in working with its beautifully glowing colors. A strand of silk thread has a smooth luster and pulls easily through the layers of the quilt. Silken threads slip their knots easily, so be sure to fasten them well.

Silk embroidery threads: Usually imported from Spain or India, these shining threads may be used for quilting if they are colorfast and strong enough. Again, fasten your knots carefully.

Wool yarns: Wool yarns are traditionally used when quilts are tied rather than quilted. However, yarn is usually not as strong and durable as crochet thread, which is a better choice for knotting.

Synthetic threads: Tangles and frustration are inevitable, in my experience, when quilting or hand sewing with synthetic threads. With so many wonderful cotton threads available, why fuss with the synthetics?

105

Wax

Running a piece of beeswax, paraffin, or candle down the length of an unruly thread will aid greatly in preventing tangles and knots. Many commercial quilting threads are already coated with wax or silicone to make sewing easier.

Thimble

A proper thimble on the middle finger of your sewing hand will be of great help as you push the needle through the several layers of the quilt. The thimble should fit the middle finger tightly enough to stay on by itself, and it should have deeply defined indentations to catch the needle. Choose a thimble without a ridge at the base, because a ridge will rub against the adjoining fingers in an irritating way.

A well-crafted thimble may cost five or ten dollars and is far different from the clumsy dimestore version with which you may already be familiar. Fine antique thimbles of silver, gold, or brass look like jewelry and are priced accordingly. They are delightful tools because they were actually designed to help in sewing. If you have one, treasure it.

Pins

The longer the pin, the more usable it will be in penetrating the several layers of the quilt. Choose rustproof pins if possible, because sometimes a quilt is left pinned for a lengthy period during its quilting.

Scissors

Sewing shears are needed for cutting fabric; a smaller pair is more useful for cutting threads while quilting.

Tailor's Chalk

Quilting lines may be drawn on the quilt top with tailor's chalk or a sliver of soap. When you are finished quilting, the chalk marks can be removed with a clothing brush or a dry washcloth. There are also special fabric pencils whose markings disappear when the fabric is washed.

Gripper

Sometimes the needle gets stuck in the depths of the quilt, and you may need a little traction to pull it through. An uninflated balloon or the cut-off finger of an old rubber glove can be wrapped around the needle to give you a more tenacious grip. Keeping hands clean and free of grease or hand lotion helps, too.

Templates

Used to trace quilting designs onto the quilt top, templates in many patterns are available commercially, or you can make your own out of cardboard. But you might find it easier and more fun to draw your quilting designs freehand. With a little practice, you'll find it possible to do most quilting without any markings at all.

Lighting

Good lighting is an essential tool for good quilting. The light should come from the front and from the side of your underneath arm. If the light comes from behind you or from the side of your sewing arm, you will be working in shadow.

Quilting Frame

A quilting frame is useful, but optional. There are advantages and disadvantages to using a quilting frame. The purpose of the frame is to keep all the layers smooth and orderly, without wrinkles. If quilting without a frame, you must make a constant effort to see that all the layers remain smooth, so you don't accidently sew in any wrinkles. Frames take up a great deal of space and require a posture that is tiring and confining. Quilting without a frame allows you to make smaller stitches, sit more comfortably, take your quilt to the beach, and fold it up to store it. There is certainly no need for a frame when working on baby quilts or small projects.

Ready-made quilting frames, as well as plans and kits, are advertised in all quilting magazines. Directions for a simple homemade quilting frame are given in the next section.

Small Frame or Hoop

Again, this is optional, but you may find a small frame or hoop quite helpful, as your work will be portable and easily stored, yet the area you are quilting can be kept smooth and wrinkle free. A large tapestry hoop or the newly invented plastic pipe frames are good choices.

Sewing Machine

A sewing machine is definitely optional when quilting, and I don't have much good to say about machine quilting. But I do recommend a machine for sewing on bindings.

Making a Simple Quilting Frame

The dimensions given are based on the 80- by 100-inch size of a popular quilt batting. The frame consists of two long runners covered with fabric, two shorter uncovered runners, and four C-clamps. The frame is supported on chair backs.

Materials

Boards: Two boards nine feet long and two boards seven feet long are needed. Narrow boards, perhaps one and three-fourths inches by three-fourths of an inch are fine. Take the time to choose boards that are not warped or bent. The type of wood is not important, but rough boards should be sanded.

Fabric strips: A sturdy fabric such as broadcloth or sheeting is needed for the two fabric strips that will cover the long runners. For boards of the above dimensions, each strip should be 104 inches by 8.5 inches. If using cotton fabric, the strips can be ripped rather than cut, thus ensuring that the long edges are parallel. The fabric will be fastened around the long boards, with a flap to which the quilt will be pinned.

C-clamps: Four C-clamps, bought at the hardware store, are used to hold the boards together at the corners. The clamp size depends on the depth of your boards. Two-inch clamps (that open to two inches) are suitable for boards less than one inch thick.

Staples and staple gun, or thumbtacks: For fastening the cloth strips to the boards, staples are more satisfactory than thumbtacks, though either can be used.

Additional Runners

Additional runners are optional, but they are helpful if you do a great deal of quilting. Over the years, I have made five sets of runners in different lengths. From three feet to twelve feet long, these runners can be used in various combinations for different size quilts. As the quilting progresses and the quilt is rolled, shorter end runners may be substituted. This is a help if floor space is limited.

Attach Fabric Strips to Runners

Lay a fabric strip on the floor. Center one of the nine-foot boards on top of the fabric strip so that the last inch of board at either end remains uncovered. Wrap the fabric around the board as shown in the picture. Use a staple gun or thumbtacks to fasten one edge of the fabric evenly along the edge of the board (Photo 6-2).

6-2. Center board on fabric strip and fasten edge of fabric evenly along edge.

Tightly wrap the fabric completely around the board and fasten in place. The wood will now be completely covered, with several inches of fabric left over, forming a loose flap down the length of the runner (Photo 6-3).

6-3. Wrap fabric tightly around board and staple. Several inches of fabric form a loose flap down the length of the runner.

The extra fabric is folded in to form a double flap, with the raw edge against the fabric-covered board. Iron the fold (Photo 6-4).

6-4. Fold in extra fabric to form a double flap, with the raw edge against the board. Iron the fold.

Fasten the doubled fabric to the board. Staple near the edge of the board so that the folded-under raw edge is fastened down and the doubled flap is free (Photo 6-5).

6-5. Staple through double-folded fabric near the edge of board, leaving doubled flap free.

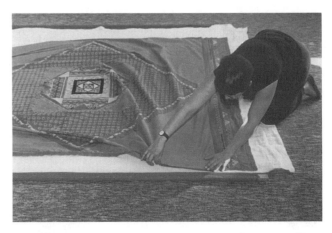

6-6. *Lay quilt top, right side up, over batting, with backing underneath. Try not to wrinkle underlying layers.*

6-7. *Put the layers in place without wrinkling. Be patient! Tug at edges to straighten.*

Cover the second nine-foot board the same way. The two seven-foot boards do not need to be covered with fabric, as the quilt will not be fastened to them. But you may wish to cover them too, so they can be used as the runners for a smaller quilt frame. Having a selection of covered runners in different sizes lets you choose a set that matches the project you are working on.

Preparing the Quilt for the Frame

Unless you have a huge table, start by sweeping or vacuuming, as it is easiest to spread the quilt out on the floor. A rug underneath will allow you to iron on the floor. Otherwise, iron top and backing before you begin, or put them in the dryer with a damp towel to get out the wrinkles.

The batting may have wrinkles or folds from being packaged tightly. You can probably pat and smooth out any wrinkles in the batting as you unfold it. A very few minutes in the dryer on the warm or delicate cycle, with a damp towel, can help smooth the batting;

but avoid using a temperature that's too hot.

Lay out the backing on the floor, making sure it is smooth and flat, with no wrinkles. If there is a right side and a wrong side to the backing fabric, place the right side facing downward, as this will be the outer surface of the underside of the quilt.

Carefully float the batting down over the backing. Raise the batting up and let it drift back down onto the backing, rather than trying to drag it into place. It is helpful to have a friend working with you, because you are handling such huge pieces of material and you must take care not to wrinkle any of the layers. If alone, be patient and handle the layers by wafting, drifting, and floating them, rather than by dragging or pulling.

Drift the quilt top down on top of the batting, right side up (Photo 6-6). As before, be careful not to drag wrinkles into the underlying layers. Socks or clean slippers allow you to walk on the quilt.

Don't be discouraged if it takes a lot of fussing to get everything properly in place. When you've got the top in

position, gently tug along the edges of the backing and batting to get out any wrinkles that may have developed (Photo 6-7).

Don't panic if there seem to be some wrinkles in the quilt top. Gently smooth, stroke, and pat the quilt top to spread any excess as evenly as possible. The puffiness that develops from quilting will eliminate most of the wrinkles (Photo 6-8).

Trim the edges so that the three layers are of the same dimensions (Photo 6-9). This is done only if a separate binding will be applied after the quilt is quilted. (See discussion of binding choices on pages 132–134.)

If you are going to bring the backing around to the front to bind the quilt, you will not want to trim the layers evenly (Illustration 6-10). The backing must be larger than the batting, and the batting larger than the quilt top.

Pinning or basting the three layers of the quilt together is an optional but very sensible step if you are using a quilting frame. If you are not using a frame, this step is essential to prevent the layers from shifting, drooping, or wrinkling. Because pins can rust and

6-8. *Gently smooth and pat quilt top to distribute wrinkles evenly.*

6-9. *Trim the batting and backing.*

snag skin or fabric, basting rather than pinning is suggested.

Make lines of basting stitches over the entire area of the quilt, spaced perhaps a foot apart (Illustration 6-11).

Really long stitches can be used for basting. Just be sure to go through all three layers of the quilt. You may find it easier to baste the quilt after it is on the frame, instead of doing it while it is spread on the floor.

6-11. *Make lines of basting stitches over the entire area of the quilt, spaced about a foot apart.*

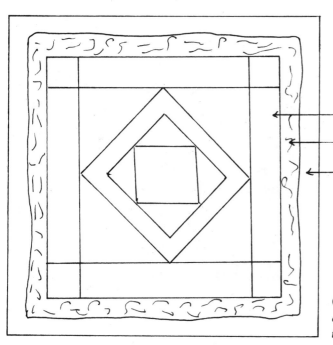

Quilt top
Batting
Backing

6-10. *If you plan to bring the backing around to the front to bind the quilt, don't trim the layers evenly.*

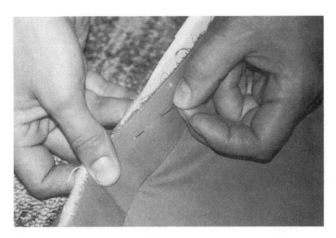

6-12. *Lay runners parallel to long sides of the quilt. Pin quilt to flaps of fabric on runners.*

6-13. *Lay ends of long runners over ends of the short runners. Then fasten the corners of the quilt frame together with C-clamps.*

Putting the Quilt on the Frame

With the quilt still on the floor, lay the two long runners parallel to the long sides of the quilt, with the folded flaps of fabric away from the quilt. Pin or sew the long sides of the quilt to the double flaps of fabric on the runners (Photo 6-12).

Position the shorter runners at the top and bottom of the quilt, with the ends of the long runners resting on top of the ends of the short runners. Fasten the corners of the quilt frame together with the C-clamps (Photo 6-13).

Don't pull the quilt tight like a trampoline. A little slack makes it easier to make small stitches (Photo 6-14).

The quilting frame in this picture is balanced on rickety doweling legs. It would be better to rest the frame on the backs of four chairs or to devise sturdier legs.

The Mechanics of Quilting

Quilting is done with a single thread, not with a doubled thread. The quilting stitch is simply a small, even running stitch that penetrates all three layers of the quilt (Photo 6-15). It will be very difficult at first to make small stitches. Remember that this is a new skill, and don't be too critical of your work. As time goes by, your stitches will get smaller.

6-14. *Don't pull the quilt too tight! Leaving the quilt a bit loose makes sewing small stitches easier.*

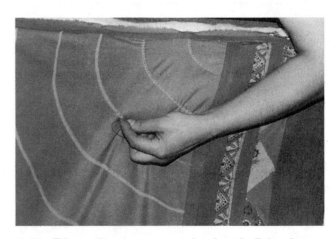

6-15. *Take small, even running stitches through all three layers.*

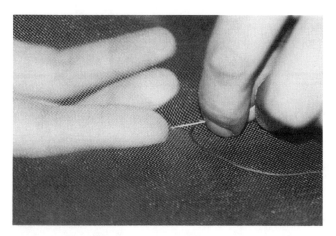

6-16. *As seen through transparent fabric, the needle should graze the finger of the underneath hand.*

6-17. *To bring the needle back up, the underneath finger presses up on the fabric that the needle is passing through.*

Hand and Needle

When you are quilting, your dominant hand (the one you write with) stays on top of the quilt to do the stitching. The other hand stays beneath the quilt. The upper hand has a thimble on the middle finger and uses it to push the needle downward. The underneath hand has two duties: to position the needle for the upward stroke and to manipulate the fabric to make the stitching easier.

Quilting Lesson on an "Invisible Quilt"

Photographs 6-16 and 6-17 show the quilting stitch being done on a transparent fabric, so that the underneath hand, which plays an active and important role, can be seen. When the needle goes down through the layers of the quilt, it is met by a finger of the underneath hand.

To bring the needle back up to the top of the quilt, a finger of the underneath hand presses up on the fabric that the needle is passing through.

When the needle goes down, you must ensure that it goes through all three layers of the quilt. To do this,

allow the needle barely to graze a finger of the underneath hand, at the same time as this finger is pressing upward just in front of the point of the needle. On the upstitch, the finger of the underneath hand pushes upward on the fabric that the needle is stitching through. Most likely, this active underneath finger will be the index finger, but it might instead be the middle finger or even the be the middle finger or even the thumb.

The thimble on the upper hand is an important tool. The little indentations on the thimble receive the head of the needle and allow you to push hard without the needle's slipping. The thimble-covered middle finger and the

thumb guide the needle downward. Two or three stitches can be taken at a time.

Repetition of these tiny finger movements propels the fabric in an up-and-down, wavelike motion just ahead of the needle, with the needle being driven through the crest of each wave (Illustration 6-18).

If the previous descriptions sound like more than you ever wanted to know about quilting, forget them and just concentrate on making a small, even, running stitch. Once you get going, your fingers will probably perform this little dance without your brain even thinking about it.

6-18. *Repeating these tiny finger movements propels the fabric in a wavelike motion just ahead of the needle, with the needle being driven through the crest of each wave.*

Fastening the Ends of Threads

Knots are generally frowned on in quilting, as they interrupt the smooth progression of stitches. Instead of knots, backstitches are used to fasten the beginning and end of each thread of stitches.

Fastening the thread: To begin, insert the needle about an inch away from where you want to start quilting. Run the needle just underneath the top fabric and come up where you want to begin stitching.

Pull the thread through until the end of it just disappears beneath the surface. This leaves an inch-long "tail" under the top fabric, which will help to keep the stitches from pulling loose (Illustration 6-19).

Take a *tiny* backstitch through the top fabric only, putting in the needle just behind where the thread comes out and bringing it back out just in front of the thread (Illustration 6-20).

Now take a longer backstitch, going through all three layers of the quilt, then begin stitching forward through all the layers (Illustration 6-21). Proceed with the stitching, until the length of thread is used up.

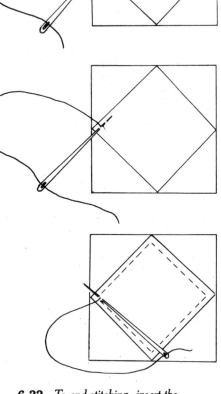

6-20. *Take a tiny backstitch through the top fabric only, putting in the needle just behind where the thread comes out and bringing it back out just in front of the thread.*

6-21. *Take a longer backstitch through all three layers. Then begin stitching forward through all layers.*

Fasten end of thread: To end a line of stitching, use backstitches instead of a knot. Insert the needle behind where the thread comes out of the fabric, then bring up the needle in front of this point (Illustration 6-22).

Then slide the needle just under the surface of the top fabric and bring it up an inch away, leaving another hidden tail underneath. Snip the thread (Illustration 6-23).

6-22. *To end stitching, insert the needle behind where the thread comes out of the fabric, then bring up the needle in front of this point.*

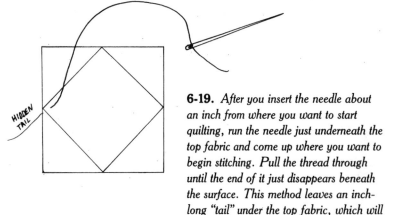

6-19. *After you insert the needle about an inch from where you want to start quilting, run the needle just underneath the top fabric and come up where you want to begin stitching. Pull the thread through until the end of it just disappears beneath the surface. This method leaves an inch-long "tail" under the top fabric, which will help keep the stitches from pulling loose.*

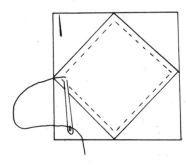

6-23. *Then slide the needle just under the surface of the top fabric and bring it up an inch away, leaving another hidden tail underneath. Snip the thread.*

Stitching

At first it may be easiest to take one stitch at a time, but soon you should be able to put two, three, or four stitches on the needle before pulling the thread through.

You will find that some directions are much easier to stitch in than others. Being left-handed, it is easiest for me to sew toward the right. So I would quilt these two sides of the square first, progressing from left to right (Illustration 6-24).

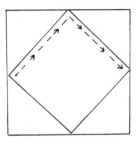

6-24. *A left-handed person would stitch from left to right, then tie knot.*

Instead of sewing "backward" from right to left, I would then begin a new line of stitching, again working from left to right (Illustration 6-25).

If you are right-handed, it would, of course, be easiest for you to stitch toward the left. See the "Troubleshooting" chapter for further discussion.

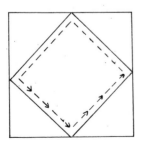

6-25. *Then begin a new line of stitching, again working from left to right.*

You can move to a different area by running the needle horizontally through the batting, underneath the quilt top (Illustration 6-26).

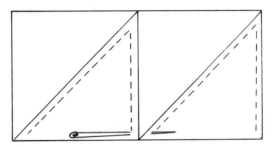

6-26. *You can move to a different area by running the needle horizontally through the batting, underneath the quilt top.*

There are three separate lines of quilting here, each running from left to right. If you are right-handed, you would find it easier to stitch in the opposite direction (Illustration 6-27).

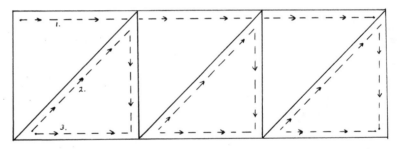

6-27. *These are the easiest left-handed stitching directions. Reverse for right-handed stitching.*

Knotting

Knots are sometimes used instead of quilting to fasten the three layers of the quilt together. A knotted quilt is not usually as durable as a quilted one, but the work certainly goes faster.

Knots can also be used to create interesting textural and visual effects, if placed to enhance the overall patchwork design. Knotting gives a puffy, tufted, comforter look to the quilt and can be used to embellish the repetitive patterns of the printed fabrics.

A repetitive pattern provides a convenient grid for spacing knots. Here, a knot will be tied through every other white flower (Photo 6-28).

Knotting and quilting can be done on the same quilt. The blue-flowered fabric in Nancy's Quilt has been knotted to give a textural contrast to the quilting (Plate 46, Nancy's Quilt, detail). It also provides a change of pace for the quilter.

Patterns of dimples can be made in the quilt top by tying the knots from the underside of the quilt or by tying the knots on the front and running the thread through the batting to hide it.

Spacing: Although people sometimes leave six or eight inches between knots, this really isn't enough to anchor the layers of the quilt strongly. These are the lumpy or tattered-looking quilts that are often found in rummage sales, having failed to withstand normal wear and washing. Knotting every two inches will add greatly to the longevity of the quilt.

Thread: A strong thread such as crochet thread or perl cotton is needed. Use a double strand instead of the single strand used in quilting. Knitting yarn, though attractive, is usually not very strong, so it is probably not a good choice.

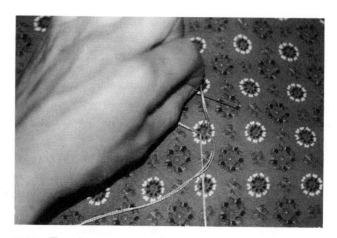

6-28. *Tying knots on every other flower makes spacing easy.*

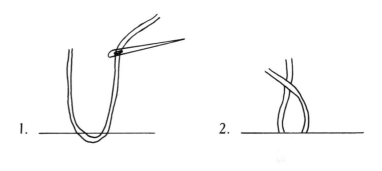

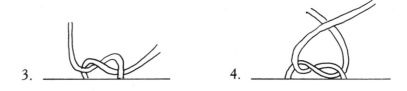

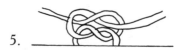

6-29. *The Girl Scout classic: right over left and under; left over right and under; pull tight.*

The square knot: This is the Girl Scout classic: right over left and under; left over right and under; pull tight. (Illustration 6-29).

1. Take a stitch through all three layers of the quilt.
2. Cross the right thread over the left thread.
3. Pass the right thread behind and over the left thread.
4. Cross the left thread over the right thread.
5. Pass the left thread behind and over the right thread. Pull the knot *tight*.

Knots in series: Sometimes called "Methodist knotting," a series of knots can be tied using half hitches as shown. Instead of cutting the thread after each knot, the thread is carried on to tie the next knot, and the next, and the next, and the next. Then the connecting threads between the knots are all cut at the same time. Strong knots can be tied at great speed using this method (Photo 6-30):

1. Take a stitch through all three layers of the quilt.
2. Take a second stitch through all the layers of the quilt, right beside the first stitch.
3. Bring the needle through the loop from behind (Illustration 6-31).
4. Pull the knot *tight*.
5. Loop the needle thread over the connecting thread.

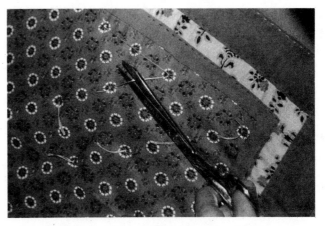

6-30. *Using this method, strong knots can be tied at great speed. Later the threads that link the knots can be cut all at once.*

1.

2.

3.

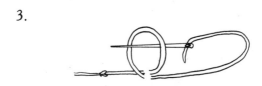

6-31. *Take a stitch through all layers. Take a second stitch beside the first. Bring the needle through the loop from the back. (Steps 1, 2, and 3)*

6. Pass the needle behind the connecting thread and over the loop (Illustration 6-32).

7. Pull the knot *tight*. (For added security, you may want to make an extra half hitch by repeating steps 6 and 7).

8. Make a chain of knots, leaving them connected by the thread.

9. Cut all the connecting threads at once (Illustration 6-33).

6-32. *Pull knot tight. Loop needle thread over connecting thread. Pass the needle behind the connecting thread and over the loop. (Steps 4, 5, and 6)*

6-33. *Pull knot tight. Make chain of connected knots. Cut all connecting threads at once. (Steps 7, 8, and 9)*

4.

5.

6.

7.

8.

9.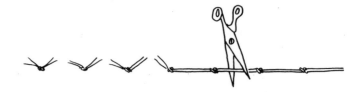

Quilting on a Frame

When quilting with a frame, you are limited to quilting a foot-wide band along the length of the runner because your underneath arm cannot reach any farther in than the elbow, unless you are a contortionist. Therefore the quilting is done in narrow bands, with the quilt being rolled up on the runners to reach a new area (Photo 6-34).

Rolling up: When you've stitched as far as you can reach, remove the needle and leave the thread hanging free. After the quilt is rolled, rethread the needle and keep stitching.

To roll the quilt, remove the C-clamps from the two ends of a long runner. Roll it up carefully (but not too tight) until you reach a fresh area. Roll it so that the quilt top is being rolled under, rather than the backing being rolled over. Replace the C-clamps (Photo 6-35).

A potential problem: There is a potentially serious problem that can develop from rolling up the quilt. The rolling stretches the quilt top tighter than the backing, causing the batting and backing to droop below the top. If you are quilting and rolling on one runner only, there will be no big problem, because you will continue quilting and rolling until you get to the opposite side, where you can then even up the edges.

But if you like to quilt symmetrically as I do, from both sides of the frame, alternately rolling up on each runner, you must be very alert to avoid a large droop of batting and backing beneath the tightly stretched quilt top.

To prevent this, with each roll of the quilt, tuck the backing in close to the runners. Careful pinning or basting will help avoid this situation. There is further discussion of this problem in the "Troubleshooting" chapter.

6-34. *Because the underneath arm can reach in only to the elbow, quilting is done in narrow bands.*

6-35. *To reach a new area, remove C-clamps, roll the quilt on the runners, and replace clamps.*

117

Stashing the frame: Unless you have a lot of floor space, you'll probably store the unfinished quilt by undoing the C-clamps and rolling it up on the runners to make a tight scroll, which can then be propped up out of the way when you're not working on it. When you unroll it later, smooth out any wrinkles that may have developed.

You might also store the quilt on the frame by leaning it up against the wall, or even suspending it from the ceiling.

It is perhaps worth mentioning that you should protect the quilt from dirt and damage during the quilting process. Keep the floor clean, keep your hands clean, keep dogs, cats, and little kids with ice cream cones away from your work. I'm in the habit of covering the quilting frame with a plastic sheet whenever I leave it.

Quilting without a Frame

Quilting a potholder, wall hanging, or baby quilt does not require a frame. Surprisingly, it is quite possible to quilt a large quilt without a frame, if some care is taken. One advantage: you can take the quilt with you to the park or to tea at the neighbor's and fold it into a bag afterward.

The main purposes of a quilting frame are to keep all the layers in order, to prevent wrinkles from being sewn in, and to organize the vast bulk of all that fabric. Without a frame, these will become your duties. You must develop a constant and unrelenting awareness of the underside of your quilt or you may immortalize big wrinkles by permanently stitching them in.

Quilting without a frame will be easiest if the quilt can be kept spread out on a large table. Baste carefully before you begin. You might find it sensible to bind the edges before you begin quilting, to prevent tufts of backing from breaking loose from the raw edges. When sewing without a frame, you must be very careful not to pull the stitching too tight. With care, quilting can even be done in your lap. Just don't sew through your skirt.

If you are hesitant to completely dispense with a frame, you'll find that a large, oval tapestry hoop or a lap-size quilting frame gives you some control over wrinkles and shifting, while still allowing portability. When you need to move the hoop or frame to a new area of the quilt, remove the hoop and spread the quilt out flat on a table or the floor. Check that all layers are smooth and unwrinkled before you put the hoop back on.

Quilting on and off the Frame

Often, I will put a quilt on the frame and quickly quilt a basic network of stitches, following the broad borders of the quilt. Then I take it off the frame, bind the edges, and do the rest of the quilting without the frame.

This two-step quilting process was used on Byzantium (Plate 17), as shown below.

On the quilting frame, broadly spaced lines of quilting stabilize the three layers of the quilt. Here, quilting follows the edges of borders (Illustration 6-36).

Once off the frame, the remainder of the quilting can be added. More elaborate quilting fills in the empty spaces (Illustration 6-37).

6-36. *Quilting of Byzantium follows the edges of the borders.*

The Logistics of Quilting

Where to Start

You can start quilting wherever you like. It may be most sensible to start at one side of the quilt and work your way to the other side, but it's not the only choice. I often start in the middle, as it's the focal point of the quilt. To be able to reach the middle, I roll up the quilt on both runners. As the quilting progresses, I unroll the quilt, alternating runners because I like to work symmetrically.

Quilt Each Seam

You may begin with a line of quilting beside each seam of your patchwork top. This greatly strengthens the seams, accentuates the patchwork, and emphasizes each border. The quilting is sometimes done right on top of the seam, but I prefer to stitch one-eighth of an inch away from the seam, so that my handiwork can be seen. Some quilters put lines of stitching on both sides of the seam, but I think quilting on one side is sufficient. There is no need to mark the stitching lines when you are following the seams; you will quickly become accustomed to stitching parallel to the seams at the proper distance (Illustration 6-38).

6-38. *Following the seams makes it unnecessary to mark the stitching lines. With practice, you will automatically stitch parallel to the seams at the proper distance.*

Fill in Empty Spaces

Because the batting may ball up in areas that are not well-quilted, quilting designs are used to fill in "empty" spaces. Try not to leave any area larger than the palm of your hand unquilted. A cotton quilt batt needs to be quilted even more closely.

Although commercial quilting templates are available to aid in marking quilting lines of scrolls, garlands, and flowers, I prefer to make up my own quilting designs, to suit my mood and the mood of the quilt. Occasionally, I'll make a cardboard template, but usually I mark the design freehand or do the quilting without marking it first.

6-37. *More elaborate quilting fills in the empty spaces of Byzantium.*

Triangles

Triangles can be divided into smaller and smaller triangles with lines of quilting (Illustration 6-39).

Quilted symbols might give an added depth of meaning. Lines can be marked with tailor's chalk or stitched freehand (Illustration 6-40).

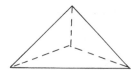

6-39. *Triangles can be divided into smaller and smaller triangles with lines of quilting.*

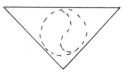

6-40. *Lines can be marked with tailor's chalk, or stitched freehand.*

Borders

Borders can be quilted with parallel lines, triangles, waves, or scrolls. Many quilt books show traditional designs you can modify. Make a cardboard pattern to trace around, or stitch freehand (Illustration 6-41).

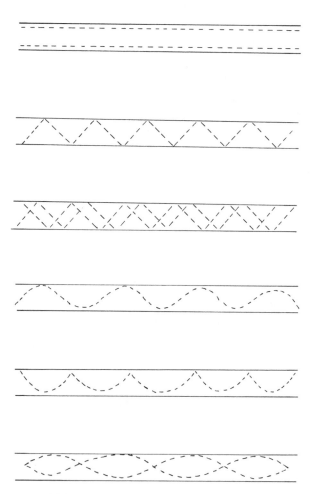

6-41. *Make a cardboard pattern for tracing, or stitch freehand.*

Corners

You'll want to invent a graceful way to turn the corners. Slightly shorten or lengthen a border motif so that it fits up to the corner. With curving lines, experiment whether a shallow or an abrupt curve moves you around the corner more smoothly (Illustration 6-42).

Sketch and Erase

You may want to sketch a possible quilting design with tailor's chalk. If you are not pleased with the result, the marks will come out if brushed with a clothes brush or a dry terry cloth towel.

Stitch and Erase

While you hope not to have to remove major portions of quilting, it is easy to erase a line of stitching you are not happy with by unthreading the needle and picking out the stitches. Then rethread the needle and try again.

Repetitive Patterns

Large expanses can be filled in by repeating a simple motif. Straight lines or a grid of diamonds are sometimes used. Repetitive patterns such as interlocking circles can be made by tracing around a saucer or similar object. The clamshell quilting in the beige and yellow background areas of the Afternoon in Paradise quilt was chosen because it echoed the shape of the starry arcs in the blue border (Plate 47, Afternoon in Paradise, detail). I used tailor's chalk to trace around a cup for the small clamshells, and I traced around a saucer for the larger ones.

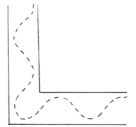
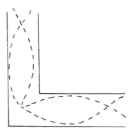
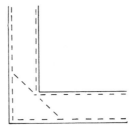
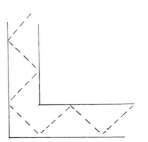

6-42. *With curving lines, experiment to determine if a shallow or an abrupt curve moves you around the corner more smoothly. Shorten or lengthen geometric lines to turn corner.*

Quilting Indecision

But what are you going to quilt where? Faced with the vast, untouched vistas of a patchwork top in need of quilting, you may be hesitant to begin.

I suggest that you start with your favorite border, even if you have to roll up the quilt to reach it. Stare at it for a minute, then trace a line with your finger. A straight line along the seam? A smoothly swooping curved line? A zig-zag? Imagine that line sketched in stitches on your border. Take up your needle and quilt it in.

6-43. *Lines and arcs can be marked using a piece of chalk on a string for a compass.*

Concentric Lines and Arcs

Concentric lines and arcs can be marked on a quilt using a piece of chalk on a string for a compass (Photo 6-43). Let out a little more string to draw each successive line.

Outline a Fabric Motif

The fabric may suggest the quilting. You might choose to sculpt and emphasize a beautiful fabric, especially in the center medallion, with detailed quilting around geometric or floral design motifs (Plate 48, Afternoon in Paradise, detail).

Trapunto

Trapunto is an ancient technique in which extra padding is forced between lines of quilting, giving an elegantly carved three-dimensional appearance to the quilt top. I highlighted the butterflies in my Yellow Butterfly quilt with trapunto by first quilting around each butterfly and then cutting tiny slits in the backing fabric (Plate 49, Yellow Butterfly, detail). I poked in bits of batting to puff up the butterflies and then sutured the slits on the back of the quilt. I don't have the patience to try the more classical method of trapunto, which avoids cutting the quilt backing by poking a hole with a blunt darning needle between the threads of the backing and forcing the batting in strand by strand.

Combine Knots and Quilting

Think of knotting as yet another quilting technique, and use it to round and soften the quilt and to accentuate the fabric design (Plate 50, Midnight, detail; Illustration 6-44, Mama's Sunflower). Alternate borders of quilting with borders of knotting.

6-44. *Mama's Sunflower (Plate 25) combines quilting and knotting.*

Doodling

The doodles you draw on the back of the phone book could become an inspired quilting design. It isn't hard to doodle or sketch with needle and thread. Lines can be "erased" by unthreading the needle and pulling out stitches. Then rethread and carry on. The blue fabrics on both the Yellow Butterfly quilt (Plate 1) and Mia's Quilt (Plate 54) are filled in with free-form quilted doodling.

Decide As You Quilt

Quilters traditionally choose a quilting design and mark it on the quilt top before they begin quilting. But quilting can be more spontaneous, with the placement of the quilting lines being decided *as* you quilt. This should be no more alarming than the decide-as-you-sew processes you followed in making medallion patchwork for your quilt top.

Choosing the quilting designs as I quilt results in more complex, unified, and cohesive designs. Equally important, having choices and decisions to make as I quilt relieves the tedium of that lengthy task.

A Progression of Stitches

I'd like to describe in detail the progression of stitches involved in the quilting of the Afternoon in Paradise quilt (See Plates 3, 4, and 5), to show how choices about quilting can be made at the moment of quilting.

I had a strong urge to quilt the brilliant flowers in the center of the medallions first, so I rolled up the quilt on both runners to be able to reach the two-foot-wide section in the middle of the quilt. Using silk buttonhole twist in colors that rivaled the flowers, I outlined the petals of each flower. I quilted the flowers in the central medallion first, then the flowers in the top and bottom medallions (Illustration 6-45).

Doing such detailed and close quilting in the three flowered squares threatened to pull the patchwork out of alignment, because the perhaps excessive amount of quilting gathered up the surrounding fabric. In order to stabilize the quilt top, I thought it best to quilt beside each seam of the patchwork. Using DMC perl cotton in colors that contrasted with the underlying fabric, I outlined the patchwork shapes in the center section. When that utilitarian task was done, I couldn't resist outlining the curious shapes printed on the blue fabric that framed the center medallion (Illustration 6-46).

The rising suns I had just quilted on the blue border made me think of using a similar design to fill in the plain background areas of beige and yellow. However, after I had sketched the design on the quilt top, I decided it was too fussy, and I erased the chalk by brushing vigorously with a clothes brush.

Instead, I chose a clamshell design, which echoed the shape in a simpler fashion. I drew around a teacup with tailor's chalk, tracing the shapes onto the beige corduroy triangles, and quilted with pink thread. I used a tumbler to mark the smaller shells on the beige border of the inner medallion and quilted with blue thread. Then I traced around a saucer for the larger shells on the yellow background and quilted with violet thread. For these larger background areas I used #30 crochet cotton instead of the more costly perl cotton (Illustration 6-47).

Having finished quilting the middle section, I undid the clamps on the quilting frame and unrolled the quilt to reach the next area of the quilt top. Again, I stitched beside each seam of the patchwork and quilted over the designs printed on the blue border (Illustration 6-48).

More clamshells were traced onto the yellow and beige backgrounds and quilted in (Illustration 6-49).

The quilt was unrolled further, to reach the outer section. The diagonal quilting of the outer borders suggested itself as an extension of the quilting along the edge of the tilted squares in one of the border fabrics (Illustration 6-50).

I then moved to the other side of the quilting frame and mirrored the stitches on the other side of the quilt.

The results of my decide-as-you-quilt stitching were very satisfying to me, combining vigor, harmony, and wit into a unified whole composed of innumerable stitches (Illustration 6-51).

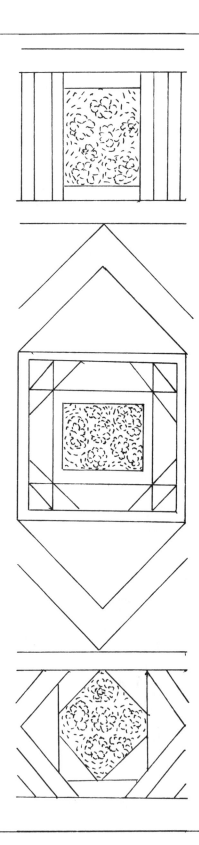

6-45. *The quilt was rolled on both runners so quilting could begin in the center. Flowers in the central medallion were quilted before those in the top and bottom medallions.*

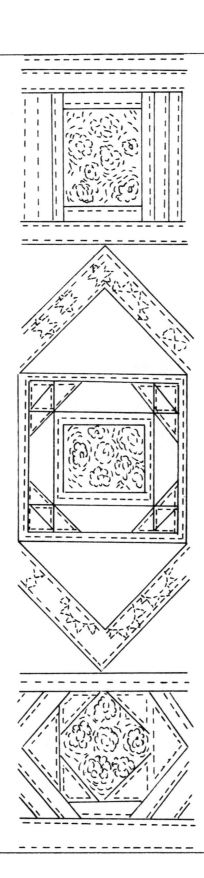

6-46. *After the floral centers were quilted, the curious shapes on the fabric that framed the center medallion were outlined.*

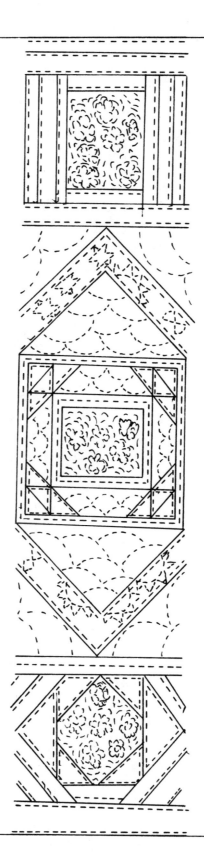

6-47. *More detailed quilting in a clamshell pattern was then added to the center. For larger background areas, try #30 crochet cotton instead of more expensive perl cotton.*

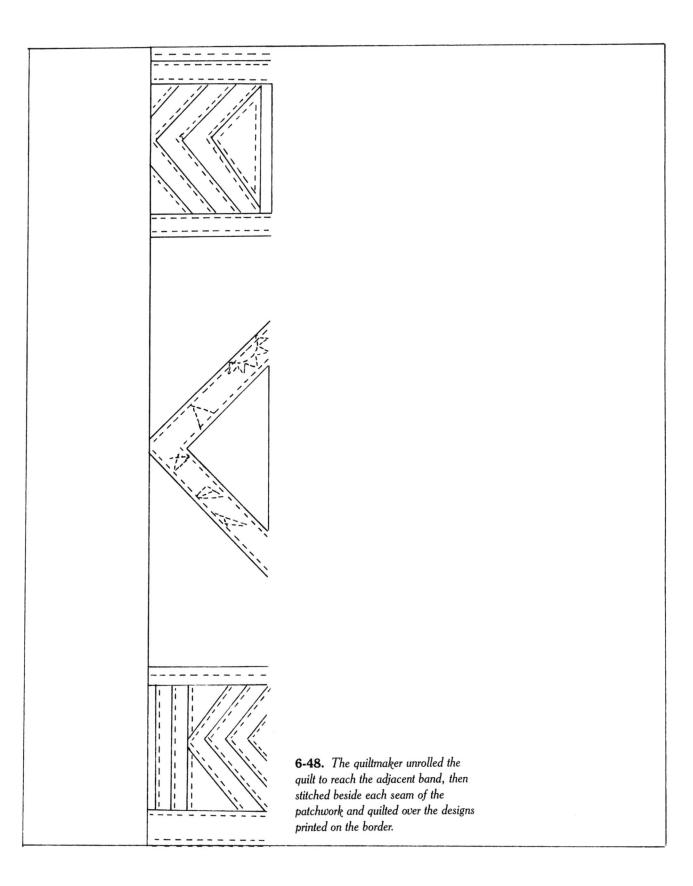

6-48. *The quiltmaker unrolled the quilt to reach the adjacent band, then stitched beside each seam of the patchwork and quilted over the designs printed on the border.*

6-49. *More clamshells were traced and quilted.*

6-50. *The quilt was unrolled further to reach the outer edge. The diagonal quilting of the outer borders suggested itself as an extension of the quilting along the edge of the tilted squares in one of the border fabrics.*

6-51. *Quilting was then repeated in a mirror image on the right half of the quilt. The results of decide-as-you-quilt stitching were satisfying to the quiltmaker, combining vigor, harmony, and wit.*

Aesthetics of Quilting

Although quilting has the practical purpose of holding the layers of the quilt together, it has a more noble purpose: beauty. The lines of quilting etch and sculpt the fabric and superimpose a more ethereal pattern over the matter-of-fact patchwork design.

Lines of Force

Even the softest lines of quilting have impact and force, and you may want to be deliberate in their placement. Lines can be used to emphasize and delineate, to direct the eye, to define space. Lines can suggest motion or stability. Lines can be playful or precise. Lines can draw attention toward the center of the quilt or lead it off to the edges. How do you want to draw the lines?

Retracing the Patchwork Top

Quilting lines that trace and parallel the seams of the quilt top stabilize the patchwork design by fastening it in place more firmly. The patchwork is, in a sense, enhanced but unaffected by the quilting. Nothing new is added. There is no tension, motion, or interplay between the patchwork and the lines of quilting. The patchwork stands alone, but in greater beauty than before.

The Scarlet and Violet quilt (Plate 29) and Desire's Inferno (Plate 38) are quilted along the seam lines.

Radiating Outward, Drawing Inward

Similar lines can have dissimilar effects, depending on their placement. The impact of the concentric arcs in Nancy's Quilt (Plate 22) would have been quite different with a change in orientation. Below are two other possibilities. The first directs our focus to

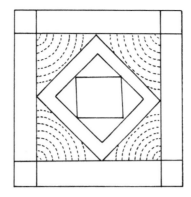

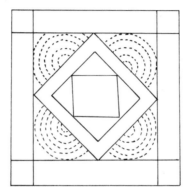

6-52. Top: *The first arc directs focus to the outer reaches of the quilt.*

Bottom: *The second draws attention to the center.*

the outer reaches of the quilt; the second draws our attention to the center of the quilt (Illustration 6-52). Combine outward and inward lines for calm but dynamic designs. The outwardly radiating lines in Ember's Quilt create fans when they cross the concentric arcs (Plate 51, Ember's Quilt). Together they enliven the plain outer borders.

Curved or Straight

Stu's Quilt (Plate 52) shows curving lines that suggest opulence and softness. Straight lines are crisp and precise. Scalloped or wavy lines give the illusion of motion or fluidity. Surprisingly, curved lines may be easier to quilt than straight ones. Another ex-

ample of straight and curved lines is found in a detail of Midnight quilt (Plate 53, Midnight, detail).

Spontaneous Quilting

Mia's Quilt is a wonderful example of freeform, spontaneous quilting (Plate 54, Mia's Quilt; Plate 55, Mia's Quilt, detail; and Plate 56, Mia's Quilt, back). Made and quilted by a strong-minded and creative group of women, it was quilted with a sense of cheerful anarchy and playfulness. Some of the quilting on Mia's Quilt is classical: tiny, uniform, ten stitches to the inch. Some of the stitching is big and wavy, three stitches to the inch. Each woman stitched in her own way. Each stitched love and affection into a special gift for a new baby and not a stitch is out of place. A line of quilting might switch color midway. Quilting designs change too, depending on the whim of the quilter.

Machine Quilting

Quilting with a sewing machine sounds like a great timesaver. In reality, it can often be a very frustrating pursuit, with the results frequently not worth the effort.

Practice first on something small, and consider if you want to cope with shoving the bulk of a large quilt repeatedly through the narrow space between the needle arm and the body of the sewing machine.

Scrupulously pin or baste before you begin. Use a long stitch. Folding or rolling the quilt into a long scroll may help in feeding it through the machine. Position a bench or table beside the sewing machine to help support the weight of the quilt.

Use your fingers actively on either

side of the presser foot, and keep the focus of your attention ahead of the needle so you have time to ease in the inevitable wrinkles. To prevent wrinkles, you will need constantly to ease the excess of fabric under the needle in tiny little gathers. The top fabric will tend to buckle or fold over seam lines, so you may be better off outlining the patchwork shapes instead of crossing seam lines. Remember that it is going to be hard to turn the quilt more than a quarter turn when you change direction.

Be extremely conscious of the underside of the quilt at all times, checking often to be sure that wrinkles or folds are not developing unnoticed on the backside of the quilt.

The finished quilt will have a different feel from one that is hand stitched. A machine-quilted quilt will be stiffer and somehow flatter, without the beautiful suppleness and grace of a hand-quilted one.

I find machine quilting useful on occasion, for small projects. But machine quilting a large quilt is such an awkward and cumbersome task that I don't find it to be worth the bother. If you want to try it, perhaps you should read a book on machine quilting written by someone with greater success and a more positive attitude toward this method of quilting.

The birds in the center medallion of the Bird Star quilt are sculpted and outlined with machine quilting (Plate 57, Bird Star, detail). This quilting was done *before* the bird square was sewn into the quilt top, because I find it is easy to do detailed machine quilting on a twelve-inch square of fabric and almost impossible to do it on a seven-foot-square quilt.

Binding the Edges

The last step in quiltmaking is to finish the raw edges. After taking the quilt off the frame, trim the edges if they are uneven. The method of binding will determine how the edges should be trimmed.

Applying a Separate Binding

A separate strip of fabric can be used to bind the edges of the quilt. Bias tape is sometimes used, but this is not a very strong fabric and may not wear well. Bias strips can be cut, but I use strips torn or cut from the straight of the grain. This binding is sewn onto the quilt in the same manner you would sew bias tape in dressmaking.

1. Trim the edges of the quilt top, batting, and backing, so all three layers are exactly the same size.
2. Cut or tear four binding strips of fabric one and one-fourth inches wide. Wider strips can be used if you wish. Two of the binding strips should be the same length as the long sides of the quilt; the other two should be several inches longer than the short sides of the quilt. Be generous and add a few extra inches to each strip in case you measured wrong; the extra length can be trimmed off later. Unless you want to cut the strips lengthwise down two and one-half yards of fabric, you will piece the strips together from several shorter lengths.
3. Iron under a quarter-inch fold for the hem along one edge of the binding strip (Illustration 6-53).
4. Line up the unfolded edge of the strip of binding with the raw edge of the quilt, right sides together. Position the strip down the length of the quilt, pinning every few inches

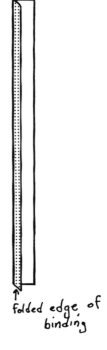

folded edge of binding

6-53. *Iron under a quarter-inch fold for the hem, along one edge of the binding strip.*

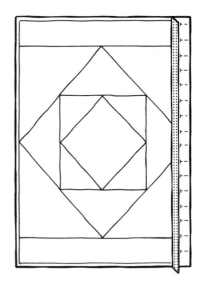

6-54. *Line up the unfolded edge of the strip of binding with the raw edge of the quilt, right sides together. Position the strip down the length of the quilt, pinning every few inches through all three layers.*

through all three layers (Illustration 6-54).

5. Stitch the binding strip to the quilt with a quarter-inch seam, sewing through all three layers of the quilt (Illustration 6-55). Iron open.

6. Attach the binding strip on the opposite side of the quilt the same way. Iron open.

7. In the same manner, attach the binding strips to the top and bottom of the quilt. Extend the ends of the strip over the side binding strips (Illustration 6-56).

8. Bring the binding over the raw edge, to the back of the quilt. Position the folded edge of binding so it hides the line of stitching. Pin binding in place, then hem. I usually make a knot every ten stitches, to add strength to the hem (Illustration 6-57). The binding can be mitered at the corners, but it is easier to fold them square, similar to the hem at the corner of a shirt front (Illustration 6-58).

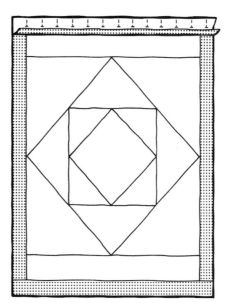

6-56. *Attach the binding strips to the top and bottom of the quilt. Extend the ends of the strip over the side binding strips.*

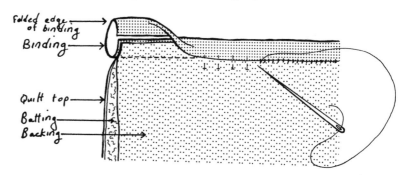

6-57. *Making a knot every ten stitches strengthens the hem.*

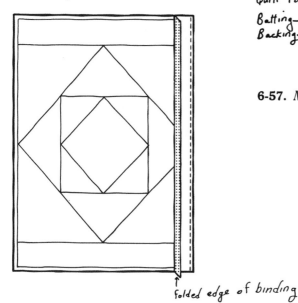

6-55. *Stitch the binding strip to the quilt with a quarter-inch seam, sewing through all three layers of the quilt.*

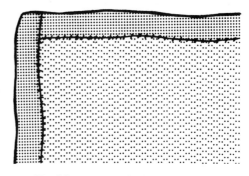

6-58. *You can miter the binding at the corners, but it is easier to fold them square, similar to the hem at the corner of a shirt front.*

Binding with the Backing

A different method of binding is to fold over the backing and hem it onto the quilt top. Because the backing fabric will thus become the last border of the medallion, choose a fabric that will enhance the patchwork top. This method can only be used if the backing and batting are larger than the quilt top.

Dimensions will vary depending on the width of the finished binding. For example, if you want a finished binding one-inch wide, the batting should extend one inch beyond the quilt top on all sides, and the backing should extend one and one-fourth inches beyond the batting on all sides. Begin by trimming the edges, so each of the three layers of the quilt is of the correct dimensions.

1. Iron under a one-fourth-inch fold for the hem along each of the four edges of the backing.
2. Bring the edge of the backing over the batting and the quilt top, aligning the fold so the raw edge of the quilt top is overlapped by one-fourth inch.
3. Pin carefully.
4. Hem by hand or machine (Illustration 6-59).

An Old but Good Binding Method

Our quilting ancestors sometimes finished their quilts with a very long-wearing and utilitarian method. The Antique Star quilt (Plate 45) was bound by turning and stitching the strong muslin backing over the quilt top. Then, a strip of brown calico was attached as a second binding over the first. This provided a dual layer of fabric where the quilt receives the most wear. Many years later, the muslin binding can be glimpsed through the tattered calico binding, but the quilt is still serviceable as the batting does not show through.

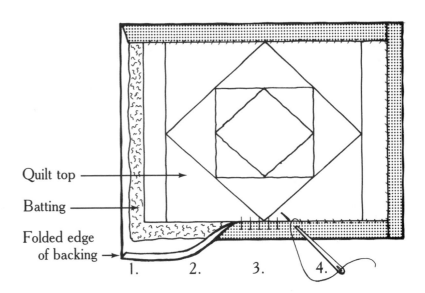

6-59. *The backing can be folded to the front. Hem by hand or machine.*

Quilt top

Batting

Folded edge of backing

1.   2.   3.   4.

Last Details

Tidy Up

You'll be looking closely at your quilt while you are quilting, so tidy up as you work. Clip off any loose threads, and brush away lint and fuzz. If you notice any seams coming loose, don't ignore them. Use your tiniest hidden stitches to mend any flaws.

Label It?

If the quilt has special washing or cleaning requirements, write this information on a square of cloth with indelible ink and stitch it to the back of the quilt. You might like to make a label with other kinds of information as well, such as the origin of the design, the source of special fabric, or historical documentation that might be of interest in years to come. There is nothing immodest about documenting your work; you have surely looked at an old quilt before and wondered about its story. If quilts could talk....

Signing Off

Use your last stitches to sign your name and the date (Plate 58, Louie's Quilt, back). If you are hesitant to do this, let the words of Averil Colby (*Patchwork Quilts*) persuade you:

Signing and dating a present-day work is an important part which is omitted all too often, and modesty on this score should be overcome for the sake of posterity. A patchwork bedspread should be a record of contemporary textiles, and as such is incomplete without the year of making, at least.

Troubleshooting

When things go wrong, there are generally a number of possible solutions. I'm offering some of the remedies I've used when my quiltmaking has gone awry. These are not definitive answers; you will begin to think up your own solutions once you accept that mistakes are not necessarily disasters.

Patchwork Problems

Problem: Running out of a Particular Fabric.
Solutions:

1. Substitute something else: Either do this subtly, by choosing the fabric that matches most closely and hope that no one will notice; or do it blatantly, choosing a different fabric that will send your design off in a new direction.

For example, the outside borders of the Afternoon in Paradise quilt (See Plate 3) are each made of different fabrics, because I didn't have enough of any one fabric for all four sides.

When I was making the Yellow Butterfly quilt (Plate 2), I imagined surrounding the central medallion with the butterfly fabric, but found I didn't have nearly enough to go around completely. The solution was to sew the four plain blue squares in the corners.

Substituting a different fabric often adds elegance and interest to the design, so don't panic if you run out. Being forced to improvise almost always produces a more intricate and creative design.

2. Skimp by with what you've got: Sometimes, narrower seam allowances will do the trick. Or you could cut narrower strips or smaller triangles.

More than once, I've taken three or four tiny snippets of a nearly extinct fabric and painstakingly pieced them into a three-inch triangle I couldn't do without. If you study old patchwork quilts closely, you will see that our frugal and practical ancestors quite often pieced a triangle out of several smaller bits of fabric.

Routinely, I splice short lengths of fabric to make a longer border strip. Sometimes I try to match the motifs on either side of the seam, but if the fabric is scarce, I don't bother.

Troubleshooting, as the name implies, refers to locating problems or faults, analyzing what is wrong, and then remedying the situation.

—Miner Brotherton, *The Twelve Volt Bible*

Problem: As the medallion grows, it gets crooked, or one side gets longer than the other, or the square is no longer a true square.

Solutions:

1. Prevention: Meticulous marking, measuring, and sewing is, of course, the answer. If your squares and strips are cut with exactness and your seams are a precise one-fourth inch, you shouldn't suffer from this problem.

Even if you are of a less meticulous nature, you may want to check the dimensions of the medallion periodically with an L-shaped framing square or a yardstick.

Pick the side of the medallion that seems most correct and lay one leg of the framing square along it. Draw lines on the fabric along both legs of the framing square. This will give two sides that are true. Then lay one leg of the framing square along one of the lines you just drew, and draw a line on the fabric along the other leg. Repeat one more time to mark the fourth side. Then trim the medallion where you marked it (See Illustration 7-1).

A more low-tech method is to measure across the medallion at top and bottom with a yardstick. If one end of the quilt is wider than the other, trim off the excess. Then turn the quilt ninety degrees and measure across it again, trimming if necessary.

2. Ignore it: This is my forte. I can easily overlook a border that is a bit wobbly or a square whose sides are not parallel. I trust that the overwhelming splendor of my quilt will keep the eye from resting on these trifling defects, and this has usually turned out to be true.

However, on occasion I have felt that a little more care in construction

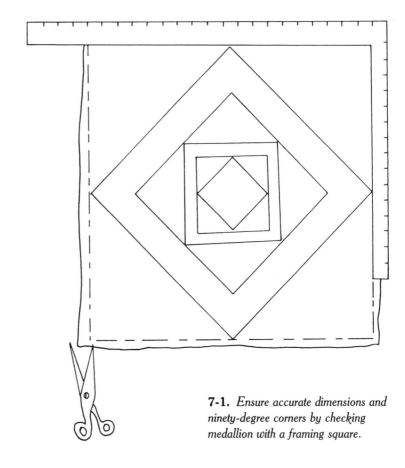

7-1. *Ensure accurate dimensions and ninety-degree corners by checking medallion with a framing square.*

would have produced a more satisfying quilt. I once gave away a quilt top rather than selling it because I had carelessly allowed it to get about ten inches wider at the top than at the bottom, and I was too embarrassed to take money for it. After that, I tried to be a little more precise.

3. Correct it: If the dimensions are just a tiny bit off, placing the next border a little askew in the opposite direction will usually correct the problem.

Another way to handle a medallion that's not quite square or true is to surround it with a broad border of triangles. Because there will be ample background behind it, slight irregularities will be overlooked.

If the problem is not noticed until the quilt top is finished, it's much harder to correct, because you've built in the defect by this time. If you can pinpoint the border where the dimensions first went awry, you may be able to sew a new, more accurate seamline that will bring the medallion back to the correct shape.

Mark the correct position of the seamline with chalk (line A). Then mark the old seamline (line B). By matching up these two lines and sewing along them so the excess fabric is hidden within the seam, the problem is corrected (Illustration 7-2). In effect, you are forming a long, narrow dart that takes in the unwanted fabric.

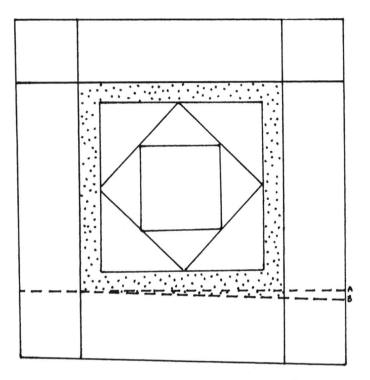

7-2. *Line A represents the correct seamline, while Line B represents the old seamline. By matching up these two lines and sewing along them so the excess fabric is hidden within the seam, you correct the problem.*

Problem: After sewing on a border, you find that the lighter fabric is a little gathered or puckered, and the quilt top doesn't lie flat anymore.
Solutions:

1. Press vigorously: Use a steam iron or give it a spray first.

2. Don't worry about it: Once the quilt is quilted, minor defects of this kind tend to disappear because of the puffiness of the batting and because the quilting gives a three-dimensional effect anyway.

3. Rip out the seams and try again: This time, smooth the two fabrics very carefully, then iron them and pin at frequent intervals. Perhaps you should check the tension on your sewing machine as well.

4. Stuff it: This is another situation where a defect can lead to a more exciting design. The baby quilt, Sweet Baby Jane (Plate 23), gains a little design drama by padding several of the outer borders. Ignore the puckering for the moment, and continue adding borders. When you are ready to quilt, put extra batting under the puckered borders and loosely stitch this extra batting to the quilt batt to hold it in place. Then quilt on either side of the raised border to anchor it firmly. By raising some borders above the surface of the quilt, you create an unusual sculptured quilt.

Problem: When sewing patchwork units, sometimes the corners of triangles don't meet precisely:
Solutions:

1. Decide whether this really presents a problem: This defect is most noticeable and annoying in the center of a medallion or patchwork unit and should probably be corrected, because the eye will focus readily on it. Mismatches at the edges of the medallion or patchwork unit are less bothersome because the eye tends to overlook them as it views the overall design.

2. Correct by ripping seam and restitching: This time, put a pin straight through both pieces at the exact spot where they must match, then carefully pin the seam (Illustration 7-3).

3. Cut out your patchwork shapes more carefully: If you consistently have this problem, perhaps your triangles and other patchwork shapes should be cut more precisely.

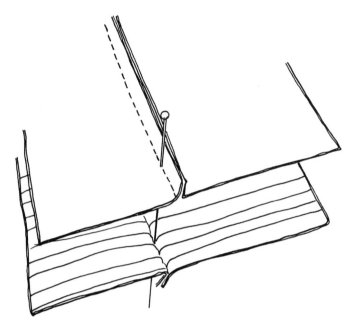

7-3. *Put a pin straight through both pieces at the exact spot where they must match and pin the seam carefully.*

Problem: When two triangles are sewn together to form a square, the square doesn't lie flat afterward.
Solutions:

1. Change the orientation of the triangle to the grain of the fabric: When the long side of the triangle is on the bias of the fabric, it tends to stretch and curve a little. When the two triangles are sewn together, a curved surface results.

If the long side of the triangle is oriented to the straight grain of the fabric, the seam that joins the two triangles will then be straight.

2. Correct the curve: If a triangle shows a slight curve, you can mark a straight line with a ruler, and then trim off the curve (Illustration 7-4).

3. Use more tightly woven fabric: This problem occurs because the fabric is a bit stretchy or loosely woven. Choosing more tightly woven fabric will help prevent this.

4. Pad underneath before quilting: Again, a defect can be used sculpturally. Put a pyramid of batting under the square on top of the batt, then baste the piled up batting to the batt with loose stitches. Quilt around the puffed up square.

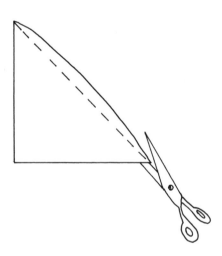

7-4. *To correct a slight curve, mark a straight line with a ruler and trim.*

Problem: When I sew triangles together to form a long patchwork band, I can't get the edges straight.
Solutions:

1. Keep trying: My patchwork bands often don't come out straight either, even after all these years of quilting.

This problem has something to do with the difficulty of judging the exact size of the little ears that are left sticking out on either side when two triangles are laid together before sewing the seam. When you are adding a triangle to a band already sewn, only one ear is visible because the other is involved in the previous seam allowance. Therefore its position is hard to judge (Photo 7-5).

2. Prevention: Judging the proper placement is even harder if the triangles have been cut out inaccurately. Dreary though it sounds, you may want to take more care in cutting out the triangles, in order to avoid problems in sewing them together.

3. Deal with the unevenness: Because it goes against my nature to be too persnickety, I tend to accept a fair amount of unevenness in my patchwork borders (Illustration 7-6).

If there is a tremendous jog between two triangles, I might rip out the seam and reposition it. But more typically, I will sew the uneven border onto the medallion, being careful to have a minimum quarter-inch seam. This means a slight narrowing of the border, as you will have a seam greater than one-fourth inch on the rest of the triangles (Illustration 7-7).

The finished border will be a little fuzzy, because the points of some of the triangles have been lopped off, but I seldom feel that this detracts seriously from the design.

7-5. *As you add triangles to a band, offset their placement so that they will match up after you sew the quarter-inch seam.*

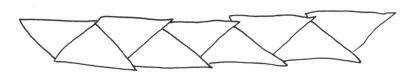

7-6. *Only you can decide how much unevenness you will accept in your patchwork borders.*

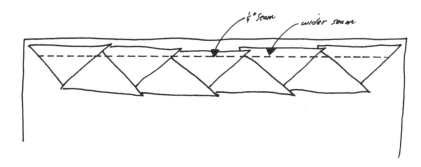

7-7. *If the jog between two triangles is great, try sewing the uneven border onto the medallion, with a quarter-inch seam at that spot. This will narrow the border slightly, because you will have a seam greater than one-fourth inch on the rest of the triangles.*

Problem: When I'm making a patchwork border, I can't figure out how many triangles I'll need for the patchwork border to fit the medallion exactly.
Solutions:

1. *Measure and calculate precisely, using traditional patchwork techniques:* Get a good classic patchwork book and follow the instructions for measuring and graphing. Be sure to add quarter-inch seams to each piece.

2. *Take a good guess; experiment; fudge a little:* I usually make up a patchwork border that I think will probably fit, and then make adjustments as necessary. I begin by laying the triangles around the medallion, letting them overlap the amount I think will be taken up by the seam allowances. I then sew the triangles together and try out the border to see if it fits. If it doesn't I'll use one of the strategies discussed below.

3. *Give it a tug or a shrink:* Minor adjustments can be made in the length of a patchwork band by pulling on it gently to lengthen it a bit, or by ironing it to shrink it. To shorten a band by ironing, bunch it up a little so it is the desired length, then spray it and press it. Although it doesn't always work, it's worth a try before you resort to a more radical remedy.

4. *Adjust the medallion to fit the band:* If the band is too short, it may be easier to trim the medallion to fit the band (Illustration 7-8).

If the band is too long, consider adding a border to the medallion to make it an appropriate size (Illustration 7-9).

5. *Chop off the ends of a band if it's too long:* Because the eye focuses on the center of the quilt, a shortened patchwork band is seldom noticed.

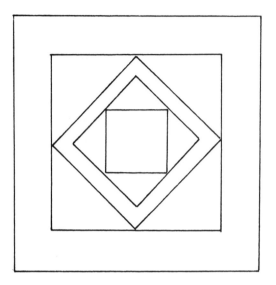

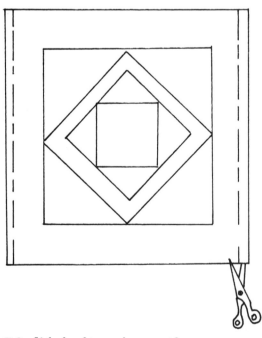

7-8. *If the band is too short, consider trimming the medallion to fit the band.*

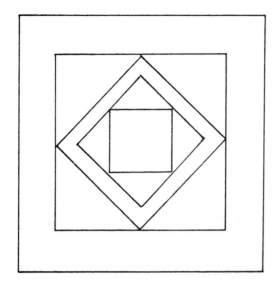

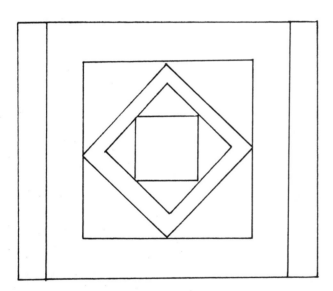

7-9. *If the band is too long, consider adding a border to the medallion to create the proper size.*

6. Adjust a few seams: You don't have to re-do every seam in the patchwork band; resewing one or two seams will usually do the trick. If you need more length, rip out the seam and sew it with a narrower seam allowance. If you want to shorten the band, sew a wider seam allowance.

Problem: When the patchwork bands are sewn on, the pattern is disrupted where the bands meet at the corners.
Solutions:

1. Don't worry about the corners: As you've probably guessed, this is often my solution, especially if the patchwork bands are not prominent in the overall design. For example, the bands of patchworked triangles on the Yellow Butterfly quilt (Plate 2) meet quite randomly at the corners, so each corner is different. I'm rather fond of the tiny hint of asymmetry imparted to the design and have never considered these mismatched corners a defect.

2. Take care at the corners: In other quilts, where I'm relying on patchwork bands to orchestrate the design, I pay a lot more attention to how the corners meet. For example, in the Scarlet and Violet quilt (Plate 29) and in Nancy's Quilt (Plate 22) the patchwork borders are prominent in the design, and I tried to turn the corners gracefully. I often use the methods described below when I want tidy, matching corners but don't want to do precise calculations or planning.

3. Work on getting the corners perfect, then adjust the medallion to fit: Lay out the patchwork border strips so they meet perfectly at the corners, remembering to allow for a seam allowance where they meet; then either trim the medallion smaller or add another border to make the medallion larger.

4. Overlap the triangles the same amount: You can make major adjustments to the length of patchwork bands *and* create tidy, symmetrical corners by overlapping the two triangles the same amount where they meet at the corners. This can be a tiny overlap or one that almost swallows up the triangles. The secret is, again, to leave little ears of the same size sticking out on either side of the corner. Trim off the ears after the border is sewn on (Illustration 7-10).

5. Add a filler at the corners: Fitting in an additional patchwork piece at the corners takes a little fussing, but it handles the situation gracefully (Illustration 7-11).

6. Cover up the corners: Sew triangles over the gaps at the corners (Illustration 7-12).

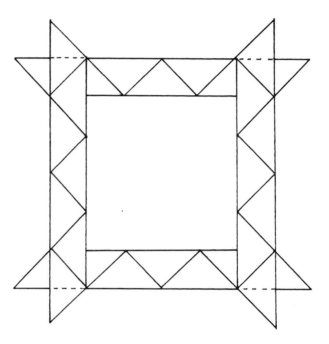

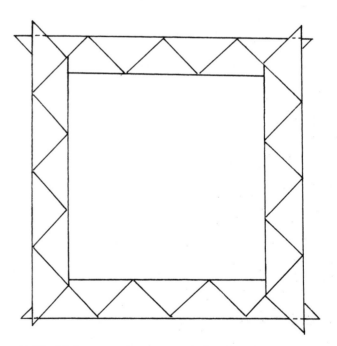

7-10. *Make major adjustments to the length of the patchwork bands and create symmetrical corners by overlapping the two triangles the same amount where they meet at the corners. This can be a small or large overlap. Make sure you leave little ears of the same size sticking out on either side of the corner. Trim off the ears after the border is sewn on.*

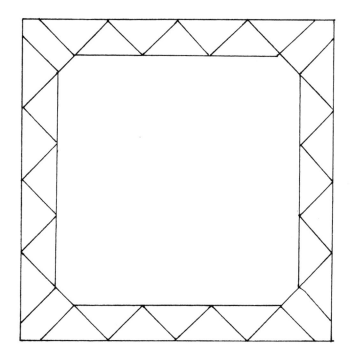

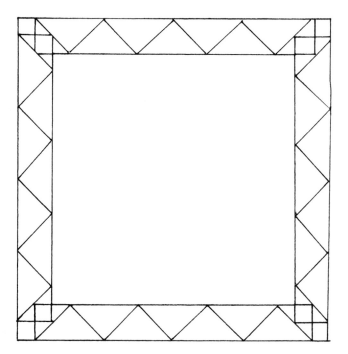

7-11. *Adding a patchwork piece at the corners can be tricky, but it solves the problem of disrupted patterns at the corners.*

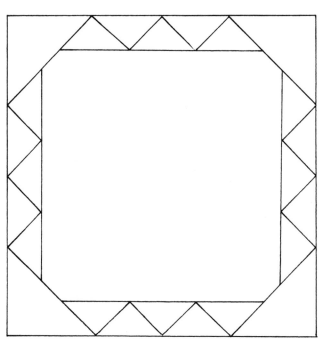

7-12. *Another way to handle disrupted patterns at the corners is to sew triangles over the gaps at the corners.*

Problem: After the quilt was finished, I hung it on the wall and found there was one fabric in it that really bothered me. Now I'm not pleased with my quilt.
Solutions:

1. Sew something else on top of it: If the quilt is completely finished, the new fabric will have to be sewn on with tiny, hidden hand stitches.

If you are sewing a new fabric onto an unquilted top, probably the first seam can be done by machine, and the rest of the sewing done with hidden hand stitching.

2. Try to pinpoint what it is that you don't like about the fabric: If you just plain don't like it, it's better to cover it up. But if you do like the fabric itself, yet find it jarring or peculiar in the quilt, it may be that there is *too little* of this fabric, so it looks out of place. You might be able to tie it into the quilt by using quilting thread the same color as this fabric. You might try appliquéing a few more patches of this fabric onto the quilt top. If the quilt is still unfinished, the easiest and most effective solution may be to add a border of the bothersome fabric so that it plays a more integral part in the design.

3. Prevention: Every time you sew a new border onto the medallion, hang it on the wall and study it. If there is something you don't like, it is easier to change it now than when the quilt is done. Because quilts get so big, and we work so close to them, we need to move away from them to see them better.

Quilting Difficulties

Problem: Thread keeps tangling and knotting.
Solutions:

1. Give yourself a fighting chance: Use a shorter thread, no longer than sixteen inches. Wax the thread by running it across a piece of beeswax, paraffin, or candle; or use a silicone-coated cotton thread. Don't use synthetic threads for hand sewing.

Untangle a snarly thread by letting it dangle with the needle near the end of it, and it will untwist itself. Or run the thread through your fingers, to help it untwist.

2. Pick or snap a knot loose: You can try picking a knot with a needle to see if it will come loose. But most knots will come free by holding the thread on either side of the knot and pulling sharply with a quick snap.

3. Cut and re-knot: For really stubborn knots, cut the thread on either side of the knot, then unravel enough stitches to allow you to rethread the needle. End the line of stitching with a backstitch, and then run the needle under the quilt top for an inch to hide the thread. Resume stitching with a new thread.

Problem: You can't get the needle threaded.
Solution:

Use a bigger needle, or try again: Try cutting the thread cleanly, on a slight diagonal. Lick the end and squash it flat by pulling it through your front teeth. Align the flat end of the thread with the long dimension of the needle's eye. My father refers to Mark Twain's method, which advises one to bring the needle toward the thread, not the thread toward the needle.

Problem: The needle gets stuck in the quilt and can't be pulled through.
Solution:

You need traction: Keep your hands clean and free of oil or hand lotion. Use a gripper made from a piece of balloon or a bit of rubber cut from a rubber glove.

Problem: The thread frays and wears through at the needle's eye.
Solutions:

1. Change technique: Every five or ten stitches, slide the needle an inch farther down the thread so it doesn't always rub at the same place. Use a shorter length of thread.

2. Change thread: Your thread may be too fragile for quilting. Use a stronger thread with a tighter twist.

Problem: Stitches are too big.
Solutions:

1. Don't be so hard on yourself: Small stitches take a lot of time and practice. Give yourself a year or two of hand stitching before you get too critical.

2. Loosen up the quilting frame: The quilt should not be stretched taut like a trampoline. Allow some slack, so the quilt dips down below the frame a few inches. This lets you move the fabric with your underneath hand, letting you take smaller stitches.

3. Quilt without a frame: Getting rid of the quilting frame, though it may introduce other problems, is the answer if you aim for tiny stitches. Without the frame, the fabric can be manipulated more easily, allowing smaller stitches.

Problem: Stitches are too crooked or uneven.
Solutions:

1. Keep practicing and don't be overly critical: If this is a new skill, it might take awhile to master it. If you've been quilting awhile and are still wobbly, ask a more experienced quilter for advice.

2. Corrective measures: You can erase a line of stitching by unthreading the needle, pulling the stitches loose one by one until the mistake has disappeared, then rethreading the needle and resuming your stitching.

If the spacing of your stitches is irregular, use a backstitch to fill in the gap, then glide the needle underneath the fabric to come up in position for the next stitch.

Problem: Needle is lost in quilt.
Solutions:

1. Keep looking: Don't risk leaving a needle in the quilt for the innocent sleeper to discover, especially in a baby quilt. Look for a lost needle by ducking down so the surface of the quilt is at eye level. Feel for the needle by gently squeezing the quilt or by brushing your hand back and forth across the quilt top. Chances are, you'll run into it.

2. Needle control: Don't leave a needle in the quilt when it is rolled up or stored between quilting sessions. End the line of stitching, or slip the needle off the thread, leaving the thread to be rethreaded later.

Try to develop the habit of always putting your needle in the same place — but not in the quilt.

Problem: Sore fingers.
Solution:

Protective strategies: Always wear a thimble on the middle finger of your sewing hand, and use it to guide the needle. Make a flexible leather thimble for your underneath hand by cutting the tip off an old glove.

Problem: Sometimes quilting seems quite easy, at other times very hard.
Solutions:

1. Fabric selection: While top priority in choosing fabric for patchwork should be fabric that looks good in the quilt, you may want to avoid stiff or heavy fabric that is going to be hard to quilt. It definitely makes good sense to choose backing fabric that will be easy to pass the needle through. Medium-weight cotton seems to be the classic choice. Thick batting is harder to quilt than thin batting.

2. Choose your direction: The direction you are quilting makes a big difference; it is much easier to quilt toward yourself than away. The easiest direction to quilt is on a diagonal toward the elbow of your underneath hand.

Problem: The underside of the quilt is wrinkling, although the quilt top is smooth.
Solutions:

1. Evaluate: A few small wrinkles are not going to matter, but you don't want huge folds or wrinkles stitched permanently into the back of your quilt. Crawl under the quilting frame and see if you can ease out the wrinkles, distributing any excess by smoothing and patting.

2. Correct: It may be necessary to take out a line or two of stitching in order to free the wrinkle. Or it might be better to add more quilting, so the wrinkle is quilted in more tightly and lost in the stitches.

During the process of quilting, small wrinkles can be eased away, with the underneath hand distributing the excess so that a tiny bit of the wrinkle is taken up with each stitch.

3. Prevent: Basting the three layers of the quilt together will prevent wrinkles. It is important to develop a constant awareness of the underside of the quilt as you are quilting. Take an occasional peek underneath to see that all is well. Get your underneath hand into the habit of feeling out wrinkles and easing them bit by bit into the stitches.

Problem: The quilt top is nice and smooth, but the backing and batting dip way down in the middle.
Solutions:

1. Don't ignore it: This is an alarming situation and, if left untended, may require a drastic solution. If you notice the batting and the backing hanging more than a few inches below the quilt top, *don't ignore it.*

The reason the dip or droop occurs is that the quilt top is drawn tighter than the batting or backing, because the bulk of material rolled on the runners stretches the top layer of the quilt the tightest.

2. Correcting a slight droop: If you notice only a very slight drooping, pin or baste symmetrically from the center of the quilt through all three layers, distributing the excess as equitably as possible underneath. As long as the excess batting and backing is spread evenly and quilted into place, it will not be too noticeable.

145

3. Prevention: Carefully basting the quilt as soon as it is layered together will keep this problem from developing in the first place.

With each roll of the quilt on the frame, tuck the batting in close to the runners by poking your fingers into the back of the quilt, down the entire length of the runner.

The problem can be avoided entirely by quilting on one side of the frame only and rolling up the quilt only on that one runner. Even if a droop develops, any excess of batting and backing will work its way to the far side and can be trimmed off once the quilting is finished, before the binding is sewn on.

But I like to quilt on both sides of the frame to develop a symmetrical pattern, so I always roll on both runners. If this is your preferred method, then strive to develop an awareness of what's going on underneath your quilt, both by checking visually and by sensing the situation with your underneath hand.

4. Surgical intervention: Major surgery is the only solution if the problem has gone unnoticed until the quilting is almost finished. This happened to me once, on Lucy's Star quilt (Plate 43), a very elaborate queen-size quilt. I didn't notice the droop until I started to quilt the last foot-wide strip in the center of the quilt.

To my horror, when I looked under the quilt I saw a huge flap of batting and backing fabric hanging *way* below the quilt top. I couldn't face taking out and redoing all my quilting. Instead, I took the quilt off the frame, turned the quilt over, and slit the backing and batting down the entire length of the quilt. I cut away a foot-wide strip of extra batting, butted the two new edges of the batting together, and sewed them up with loose stitches. I then cut away the extra backing material, being careful to leave a good seam allowance. Very tediously, I sewed the seam together, leaving a great stark incision running the length of the backing. I never told Lucy what happened. Now she knows.

Problem: The quilting is finished, but the three layers of the quilt don't match up nicely at the edges. How will I bind it? Solutions:

1. Trimming: If the quilt top is smaller than the other layers, it is easiest to trim the batting and backing to match.

2. Adding: If the backing is skimpier than the quilt top, add a bit where needed.

If there are places where the batting is thin at the edges, take a strip of batting and loosely stitch it by hand onto the edge of the batting.

3. Binding: Cover up any discrepancies in the dimensions of the backing and the quilt top by applying a wider binding.

Problem: All I do is think about making quilts all the time. Solution: Make another quilt!

Conclusion: My Last Chance To Give Advice

At a lecture Nancy Crow, a superlatively innovative quilter, gave in Seattle some years ago, she said two words that have stuck with me ever since: "Take risks." It's hard to find better advice than this if you strive to make quilts that go beyond the ordinary. What else can I tell you?

Be as ruthless as Napoleon or Atilla the Hun in staking your claim to workspace. I started quiltmaking when I moved to a new town and a new house, so it was easy to comandeer an empty bedroom for my new craft. I was lucky the next two moves, each time nabbing a spare room. Later I found myself sharing a one-room apartment with another person and two dogs. I claimed a nook in the outside hallway for my workspace.

My next workroom was vast, fully half the floor space of a little cabin in the woods. There was no electricity, but I had a Singer treadle machine, and big windows to let in the pale northcoast sun. When I moved again, the computer got the spare room, so I set up my sewing in the bedroom. Now I quilt large projects in the living room or outside on nice days.

Quiltmaking takes space, so don't be shy about claiming a corner of your house. But don't let the lack of perfect workspace stop you either. Remember that some of those beautiful old Log Cabin quilts were sewn in small, dark cabins. Whatever your circumstances, you can at least grab the corner of a table for your sewing machine and put your box of fabric and your basket of scraps underneath it.

It's nice to be able to buy new yardage, but scraps are the real treasure. Don't throw away bits of fabric that you like. Nancy Halpern, a quilting trail-blazer, comments, "I love scraps. I am a collector. I am a salvager, I am a recycler, and I like that scrappy quality that you find in nice, old, everyday quilts." Get rid of fabric that you don't like, but save those beautiful scraps.

Don't throw away your mistakes, either. Mistakes can lead you into new design territory that you might not dare to enter otherwise. Halpern suggests, "Bite off more than you can chew, get into trouble, find interesting ways out. Relish 'mistakes.' They are probably design presents in disguise."

As expert quilter Georgia Bonesteel says, "Making a mistake is the truest form of originality." But mistakes that threaten the durability of your quilt are a different matter. Keep your tension adjusted, use strong thread, check

I must work this way, making visual judgments as I move along. I hate working from a drawing. It's too constricting.

—Nancy Crow

your seams, and keep on ironing every step of the way.

Don't be scared to mix fabrics, to let your colors clash, or to try a new approach. Ellen Oppenheimer, who makes eye-popping masterpieces, says, "Just try it. It's difficult to try something new, different, unexplored. To help myself embark on things that possibly might not work out, I remind myself that the materials I am using are not woven of golden threads."

Put your patchwork-in-progress on the wall so you can get a good look at it; keep moving the elements of the design around until the best arrangement reveals itself. Be brave. Sally Knight explains how she designs her distinctly original quilts: "I said, 'What the heck, I'm going to try new things.' I always have a plan, but it's a loose plan...I play with fabric, think about an approach. An idea may come out, and then I move on."

Don't be afraid to change the rules or to take off in a new direction. You needn't decide ahead of time whether a particular medallion will become a quilt or a potholder. Wait and see how it develops.

Let your quilting pattern develop spontaneously; adding, embellishing, incorporating new ideas as you work. Use the quilting to enhance the patchwork patterns. Dorothy Bettis, an inspired hand-quilter, explains, "Anything that you want people to see, you quilt, but you don't quilt it down. You quilt into it, you let it pop up. You quilt the background a lot so that it will sink and that way you make them see what you want them to see."

Take your quilting frame outside into the sunshine. Try a thicker, brighter quilting thread and don't intimidate yourself with unrealistic standards of perfection. But check the underside of the quilt as you stitch, and don't skimp on the quilting. "Quilting is a big, long, patient job, even a painful job...the more quilting on a quilt, the more beautiful it is," comments Bettis.

Crow says, "A quilt cannot be hurried. Solutions come in their own good time." Take your time. Take risks. Have fun.

And send me a picture of your quilt!

References: Dorothy Bettis, "Quilt What You Want Them to See," by Dianne Ridgley, *Quilting International,* Vol. 4, No. 1; Georgia Bonesteel, "A Quilter's Survey," *Quilter's Newsletter Magazine,* Dec. 1993; Nancy Crow, "The Meetin' Place," by Penny McMorris, *Quilter's Newsletter Magazine,* Dec. 1993, also lecture in Seattle; Nancy Halpern, "The Meetin' Place," by M. E. Miller-Walter, *Quilter's Newsletter Magazine,* Nov.-Dec. 1983 and "Five American Quilters," by Mary Reddick, March 1988, Sally Knight, "Sorting It All Out," by Paula Tetford Diaco and Marie Flaim Tetford, *Quilting International,* Jan. 1994; Ellen Oppenheimer, "Fabric Puzzles," *Quilts and Quilting* (Taunton Press, 1991).

Suggested Readings

This is a list of the books on my bookshelf; certainly not a comprehensive listing of the subject. Few how-to books are included, because I'm not good at following directions. I choose my quilting books by the pictures and immerse myself in the images of the quilts, wanting inspiration rather than instruction.

Books

The Perfect Patchwork Primer (Penguin, 1973), by Beth Gutcheon, is the first quilting book I ever read and is still a favorite twenty years later. It begins with a witty and insightful essay on quilting, tells you everything you need to know to make a quilt, and has four hundred and seventy drawings.

Quilts and Quilting from Threads (Taunton, 1991) contains an article I wrote for *Threads*, so it too is a favorite. It contains twenty-eight other chapters with fascinating slants on quiltmaking.

Wearable Art for Real People (C&T, 1989), by Mary Mashuta, is a gallery of wonderful patchworked clothing.

Advanced Quilting (Scribner's, 1980), by Elsie Svennas, shows hundreds of interesting projects and methods.

Double Wedding Ring (Quilt Digest, 1990), by Laura Nownes, inspired me to make a table runner with gold lamé rings for my parents' fiftieth wedding anniversary; but as with most how-to books, I had great difficulty in understanding the directions, and a lot of trouble being precise enough.

The Quilt: New Directions for an American Tradition (Schiffer, 1983), documents Quilt National 1983. Great quilts, disappointing color reproduction.

Quilts: The State of an Art (Schiffer, 1985), presenting the quilts exhibited at Quilt National 1985, is a book I've spent hours looking at; a wealth of inspiration.

The Quilt, Stories from the Names Project, is unfortunately not in my book collection. But I keep the pamphlet "The Aids Memorial Quilt" with my books to remind me of the astounding exhibit I saw of part of the 14,000 panels.

The Dinner Party, Embroidering Our Heritage, and *The Birth Project*, by Judy Chicago, are not quilting books, but they are wonderfully inspiring documents of women's creativity, so I keep them with my favorite quilting books.

Quilts, The Great American Art (Miles and Weir, 1978), by Patricia Mainardi, is a feminist essay on quilts, women, anonymity, the art establishment, and history.

Treasures in the Trunk: Quilts of the Oregon Trail (Rutledge Hill, 1992), by Mary Bywater Cross, documents the everyday life of women travelling west by wagon and links their quilts to their experiences.

Lone Stars: A Legacy of Texas Quilts, 1836–1936 (University of Texas, 1986), by Karoline Patterson Bresenhan and Nancy O'Bryant Puentes, is a favorite book of mine, for the extraordinarily vivid and energetic quilts made by women who look as though life has worn them out.

Pioneer Quiltmaker: The Story of Dorinda Moody Slade (Sanpete, 1990), by Carolyn O'Bagy Davis, tells us in detail something we too seldom know, how a woman's life and quilts are tied together.

Hearts and Hands (Quilt Digest, 1987), by Pat Ferrero, Elaine Hedges, and Julie Silber, is a fascinating and scholarly quilt history book, with exceptional illustrations that tie the themes together.

The Esprit Quilt Collection (Esprit De Corp, 1985), catalogues the company's display of vividly colored Amish and Mennonite quilts.

The Pieced Quilt, A North

American Design Tradition (McClelland and Stewart, 1973), by Jonathan Holstein, is a classic quilt book, and one of the first I owned.

Quilts and Other Bedcoverings in the Canadian Tradition (Van Nostrand Reinhold, 1979), by Ruth McKendry, offers quilts seldom seen in U.S.-oriented books and illuminates quilt history north of the border.

America's Quilts and Coverlets (Weathervane Books, 1974), by Carleton L. Safford and Robert Bishop. I've put in a lot of hours poring over this one.

Japanese Quilts (Dutton, 1988), by Jill Liddell and Yuko Watenabe, is a book I don't own but wish I did. Transplanted from the American quilt tradition, old patterns develop an enviable originality and asymmetry in Japanese hands.

Mariner's Compass (C&T), by Judy Mathieson, is filled with dizzying examples of masterpiece mariner's quilts, none of which have I attempted.

Mandala (Sudz Publishing, 1983), by Katie Pasquini, is an inspiration and a visual delight. Incredible colors, incredible quilts. I haven't tried to follow her directions for working with complex geometric shapes, but often wished I had.

Nancy Crow: Quilts and Influences (American Quilters Society), is the next book on my shopping list. Written by Nancy Crow, an industrious and innovative quiltmaker, and filled with her amazing quilts.

The Quilt Digest (Quilt Digest Press, 1983–87), edited by Michael Kile. I have one volume of this gorgeously illustrated publication, and wish I had them all.

Uncoverings, a yearly publication of the American Quilt Study Group, publishing quilt research of great variety and interest. (The 1993 volume contains a paper I wrote about the amazing women who made Mia's Quilt and twenty-eight other quilts as group projects.)

Newsletters

Blanket Statements, from the American Quilt Study Group (660 Mission St., Suite 400, San Francisco, CA 94105-4007).

Cover Stories, from the Canadian Quilt Study Group (1109 160A St., White Rock, B.C. V4A7G9 Canada).

Glossary

Appliqué: A method of creating patterned quilt tops by cutting elements of the design from different fabrics and sewing them onto a background fabric.

Baby Quilt: A small quilt for an infant, perhaps thirty-six inches by thirty-six inches, or perhaps forty by fifty inches.

Backing: A large piece of fabric, often a sheet, used as the bottom layer of a quilt.

Backstitch: A stitch taken in reverse direction to the usual direction of stitching in order to reinforce the seam or to fill in a gap in the stitching.

Basting: A temporary network of large stitches used to hold the layers of the quilt together while it is being quilted.

Batik: A type of fabric decoration that develops patterns and colors by masking portions of the fabric with wax, then dipping the fabric in dye.

Batting: The warm, fluffy insulating material used as the middle layer in a quilt. Also called "batt."

Bias: A line forty-five degrees off the straight grain of a fabric. Cutting along the bias makes fabric stretchy and flexible.

Binding: A narrow fabric strip sewn over the outer edges of a quilt, hiding the raw edges of the top, batting, and backing.

Blazing Star: A complicated, traditional quilt pattern using innumerable diamonds to create a star.

Blends: Fabrics manufactured from a mix of cotton and synthetic threads.

Block: One design unit of a traditional patchwork quilt; also called a "square."

Borders: The series of concentric shapes that compose a medallion quilt, each border being formed by sewing four strips or four triangles to the four sides of the existing medallion.

Broadcloth: A finely woven cotton fabric.

Buttonhole Twist: A very strong, tightly twisted thread that is pleasing to quilt with when made of silk, and frustrating to quilt with when made of synthetic fiber.

Calico: A cotton fabric decorated with small repeating patterns.

Carpenter's Square: An L-shaped metal ruler for precise measurement and marking.

Chenille: A highly-textured bumpy fabric with loops of thread in patterns above the surface.

Chintz: A cotton fabric with a shiny

When I use a word, it means just what I choose it to mean — neither more nor less.

—Humpty Dumpty
Through the Looking Glass

finish, usually decorated with large-scale and ornate floral designs.

Clip-and-rip: A method for making fabric strips by clipping the edge of the fabric, then ripping it.

Cotton: A fabric or a thread made from the fibers of the cotton plant; sometimes used in place of the word "thread," as in embroidery cotton.

Cut-and-fold: A method of quickly cutting triangles by folding the top of a strip diagonally, and cutting along the fold.

Decide-as-you-sew: A carefree method of quiltmaking that avoids preplanning the quilt.

Design-as-you-go: A process of quiltmaking that involves making design decisions as you construct the quilt, rather than deciding or planning before you begin.

Diamond: A configuration in medallion quiltmaking created by turning a square forty-five degrees.

Double-bed Quilt: A large quilt whose dimensions are probably determined by the size of batting available; perhaps seventy-five inches by ninety-five inches, or perhaps eighty inches by one hundred inches.

Frame: A device that stretches a quilt and holds all the layers in place while it is being quilted.

French Knot: A decorative embroidery stitch that forms raised dots.

Grain of Fabric: The edges of a fabric that lie parallel to the threads the fabric is woven from, 45 degrees from the bias.

Gripper: A bit of thin rubber or suede that can be wrapped around a needle to provide traction when the needle gets stuck.

Hexagon: A six-sided geometric shape.

King-size or Queen-size-Quilt: A ridiculously large quilt you regret having decided to make so big!

Knot: A small tangle essential to securing a line of stitching, but a mixed blessing when it occurs spontaneously. Knots can also be used to tie the three layers of a quilt together.

Knotting: An alternative to quilting; a means of fastening a quilt together by passing a threaded needle down through the layers and back up again, then tying a knot with the thread.

Layers of a Quilt: The quilt top, batting, and backing.

Little Ears: The corners of triangles that stick out when the triangles are overlapped before being sewn together.

Log Cabin: A traditional quilt pattern with two sides in dark colors and two in light, composed of concentric strips sewn around a small center square.

Medallion: A type of quilt pattern that develops by progressively adding borders concentrically around the gradually enlarging quilt top.

Methodist Knotting: An efficient method of knotting, in which a series of knots is tied before the connecting threads are cut.

Octagon: An eight-sided geometric shape.

Paisley: Fabric decorated with stylized floral designs resembling curving fronds and feathers.

Patchwork: A method of creating patterned quilt tops by cutting out innumerable small geometric shapes and sewing them together with narrow seams to form larger designs.

Perl Cotton: Strong, colorful threads usually used for crocheting; a good alternative to traditional quilting thread.

Polyester: A strong, warm, lightweight synthetic fiber used to make modern quilt batting (regrettably containing petrochemicals and sometimes formaldehyde).

Presser Foot: A foot-like attachment on a sewing machine with a space between its two "toes" for the needle. The presser foot holds the fabric in place during sewing.

Quilt Top: The decoratively patterned upper layer of a quilt.

Quilting: The network of running stitches sewn through the three layers of the quilt to fasten them firmly together.

Quilting Stitch: A line of small even stitches taken through all three layers of the quilt.

Quilting Thread: A strong thread, preferably cotton, used for quilting.

Raw Edge of Fabric: An edge that has been cut or torn and has not been hemmed or bound.

Rayon: A fabric made from cellulose fibers.

Right-angle Triangle: The shape most commonly used in medallion patchwork; an isosceles triangle with a ninety-degree corner and two forty-five-degree angles.

Right Side of Fabric: The side of the fabric you prefer to have showing; the side with the brightest colors and most clearly printed patterns.

Rotary Cutter: A wheel-shaped razor blade used like a pizza cutter to cut fabric quickly and accurately.

Rotary Cutter-strip Piecing: A way to make varied patterns by sewing together rotary-cut strips, then cutting them apart in different configurations and recombining them.

Runners: The long wooden strips to which the sides of a quilt are attached on a quilting frame.

Running Stitch: An even, repetitive stitch in which the threaded needle goes down through the fabric and comes back up a short distance away; in quilting, the running stitch pierces all three layers of the quilt.

Sawtooth Border: A traditional patchwork pattern formed by a row of triangles facing the same way, with the points resembling the teeth of a saw.

Seam: The line of stitches that joins two pieces of fabric near their raw edges.

Seersucker: A comically dignified fabric with puckered, bumpy woven stripes.

Seminole Patchwork: A method of patchwork devised by native Indians of Florida in which strips of fabric are sewn together, then cut diagonally and recombined to form elaborate patterns.

Single-bed Quilt: A reasonably sized quilt that would cover the top of a large bed or hang over the sides of a narrower bed; perhaps sixty or seventy inches by eighty-five inches.

Square: A shape that reappears concentrically enlarged in medallion patchwork; a quilt block of a uniform size that is used repeatedly in traditional patchwork quilts; an L-shaped ruler used for marking and measuring.

Strip: A long narrow band of fabric, sometimes plain, sometimes constructed from a number of small patchwork pieces.

Synthetics: Man-made fabrics, threads, and fibers; fabrics that are not made from cotton, silk, or wool; fabrics made from oil, plastic, and the chemicals used in antifreeze.

Tailor's Chalk: A type of chalk that makes temporary markings on fabric.

Tailor's Knot: A useful way of ending a line of stitching by pulling the last stitch partway through the fabric, passing the threaded needle through the loop that forms, and pulling the knot tight.

Tatting Thread: A strong, thin, cotton thread used in making a type of lace; a suitable alternative for quilting thread.

Template: A rigid form that can be traced around to reproduce accurate geometric shapes for patchwork or repetitive patterns for quilting.

Tension: A needlessly confusing sewing machine concept that signifies whether the upper thread and the bobbin thread are in correct balance; an important function to take seriously to ensure strong seams.

Thimble: A tiny, bucket-shaped metal cap worn on the tip of the middle finger; though sometimes scorned in modern times, it remains an extremely useful and necessary quilting tool.

Trapezoid: A lopsided rectangle with two parallel edges.

Trapunto: A quilting technique invented in Italy, in which extra batting is stuffed into an area outlined with stitches to sculpt the surface and bring quilting into the third dimension.

Triangle: A three-sided geometric shape; in medallion patchwork usually a right-angle triangle; sometimes used to describe a triangular template.

Troubleshooting: A way to avoid panicking by seeking innovative solutions to large problems.

Underneath Hand: Your nondominant hand, which stays beneath the quilt when quilting; your right hand if you are left-handed and vice-versa; your helping hand.

Upper Hand: Your dominant hand, which stays on top of the quilt during quilting.

Velveteen: A lovely quilting fabric, soft and richly vibrant, with a thick, short pile on one side.

Wall Hanging: A quilt, often small, which is hung on the wall.

Wax: A piece of beeswax or candle that is rubbed along the length of thread to prevent it from tangling.

Wrong Side of Fabric: The side of the fabric that you don't want to show on the outside of the finished quilt; the back of the fabric, usually duller looking than the right side.

Index

Kristin Miller is a Seattle native who lives on Digby Island across the harbor from Prince Rupert, British Columbia. A graduate of the University of Washington, she works in the mental health field. Her summers are spent on a sailboat, exploring the marine wilderness of northern British Columbia.